CASES IN BEHAVIOR MANAGEMENT

SCOT DANFORTH
University of Missouri—St. Louis

JOSEPH R. BOYLE
Virginia Commonwealth University

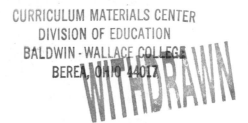

Merrill,
an imprint of Prentice Hall
Upper Saddle River, New Jersey *Columbus, Ohio*

Library of Congress Cataloging-in-Publication Data
Danforth, Scot.
Cases in behavior management/Scot Danforth, Joseph R. Boyle.
p. cm.
Includes bibliographical references.
ISBN 0-13-755711-6 (pbk.)
1. Classroom management. 2. Behavior modification. I. Boyle, Joseph R. II. Title.
LB3013.D34 2000
371.102'46dc21

99-31120
CIP

Editor: Ann Castel Davis
Production Editor: Sheryl Glicker Langner
Design Coordinator: Diane C. Lorenzo
Text Designer: Mia Saunders
Cover Designer: Paul Isaacs
Cover art: SuperStock
Production Manager: Laura Messerly
Editorial Assistant: Pat Grogg
Electronic Text Management: Marilyn Wilson Phelps, Karen L. Bretz, Melanie N. King
Director of Marketing: Kevin Flanagan
Marketing Manager: Meghan Shepherd
Marketing Coordinator: Krista Groshong

This book was set in Bookman by Prentice Hall and was printed and bound by R. R. Donnelley & Sons Company. The cover was printed by Phoenix Color Corp.

Printed in the United States of America

10 9 8 7 6 5 4 3 2 1

ISBN: 0-13-755711-6

Prentice-Hall International (UK) Limited, *London*
Prentice-Hall of Australia Pty. Limited, *Sydney*
Prentice-Hall of Canada, Inc., *Toronto*
Prentice-Hall Hispanoamericana, S. A., *Mexico*
Prentice-Hall of India Private Limited, *New Delhi*
Prentice-Hall of Japan, Inc., *Tokyo*
Prentice-Hall (Singapore) Pte. Ltd., *Singapore*
Editora Prentice-Hall do Brasil, Ltda., *Rio de Janeiro*

We dedicate this book to Dr. Tom Shea
in appreciation for his friendship, mentorship,
and three decades of passionate devotion
to the well-being of children with disabilities.

PREFACE

University students studying education and allied service fields often take courses in "behavior modification" or "behavior management." These courses are provided under the reasonable assumption that these professionals-to-be will need to know how to effectively deal with the wide range of behaviors that children and adolescents engage in. Specifically, teachers need to know how to develop and maintain a safe and peaceful atmosphere in which students can apply themselves to academic tasks and develop meaningful relationships.

Many of these university courses on "behavior management" suffer from a common weakness, a lack of thought-stirring opportunities for students to apply and discuss the behavior management theories and practices on the uncertain and multifaceted terrain of real social problems. The theories and techniques taught in the course tend to hang in the decontextualized air, leaving the student wondering what these ideas would mean if applied to actual child behavior problems that occur in schools and other settings. This book of 38 cases directly addresses that need by providing realistic, context-rich narratives of behavior problems and social conflicts which developing professionals can ponder, puzzle over, discuss, argue about, and even disagree on.

Each case consists of two parts; a quick description of the problem incident itself and in-depth coverage of salient background information concerning the individuals involved, the immediate social context, the school or institutional setting surrounding that context, and aspects of the community at large. We have attempted to provide a broad range of behavior problem situations involving children and youth of all ages and abilities, ranging from preschool settings to high schools. We have distributed the cases equally across a continuum of general and special education environments: segregated special education classes and programs, inclusive education arrangements, and general education classrooms lacking students identified with disabilities.

In addition, we have included a small number of behavior problem cases occurring beyond school settings. We have done this because often teachers are asked by parents and others to serve as consultants to help solve social and behavior problems that happen at home, at day care, at church, or at the mall. These cases are ideal for exploring the challenges of parent-teacher collaboration. All in all, our purpose has been to provide a broad array of situations, settings, and participants for your consideration and reflection.

The structure of this text is very simple. There are two introductory chapters followed by 38 cases. Chapter one gives a brief overview of social systems theory and the four basic theoretical models of human behavior and classroom management utilized by teachers. Social systems theory consists of a series of ecological rings extending from the child outward to the culture or society. It helps us to envision the many levels of social interactions, organizational structures, and cultural influences that play important roles in the creation and solution of child behavior problems. The four management theories we describe are those most commonly used by teachers: behavioral, psychodynamic, environmental, and constructivist. We cover these briefly under the assumption that university students are receiving other readings or instruction on these ideas.

The second chapter articulates a general format for case analysis that may be applied to the cases. This format includes both immediate intervention and long-term intervention. Immediate intervention is on-the-spot action taken to reduce a dangerous or threatening situation. Long-term intervention involves careful planning and action designed to help a child or group improve behavior and relationships. The chapter concludes with an example of case analysis by way of the general format and the theories we offer.

The 38 cases are arranged in random order. To help you access the kind of cases you want to address, we have provided a Cases Log (printed on the inside cover) that organizes the cases based on setting, type, and other useful variables. Our cases fall into two types: professional interventions in which teachers or other professionals attempt to design and implement an intervention intended to improve child behavior and resolve conflict, and parent-teacher collaborations in which teachers must work with parents and community members to address behavior issues beyond the school walls and grounds. There are four categories of settings where incidents take place: school classroom, school nonclassroom (e.g. hallways, cafeteria), home, and community (e.g. day care, church).

In addition, we have varied the school classroom incidents across four levels of development (school grade levels) and three forms of classroom organization. The four levels of development correspond to typical educational buildings for different age groups: preschool, elementary, middle, and secondary. The three classroom organizational types included for each of these developmental levels are special class, mainstreaming or inclusion, and general class.

ACKNOWLEDGMENTS

We would like to thank the following reviewers for their valuable input and suggestions: Jim Burns, College of St. Rose (NY); Kathleen Gruenhagen, North Georgia College and State university; Darcy Miller, Washington State University; Philip Swicegood, Sam Houston State University; and Marshall Zumberg, Wayne State Unversity (MI).

CONTENTS

PART I

BASIC PRINCIPLES OF BEHAVIOR MANAGEMENT AND USING CASES

C H A P T E R   O N E

Basics of Behavior Management

Behavior management is an array of interventions created to help teachers influence the behavior of children and teach them to behave in positive and safe ways. These interventions are designed not merely to alleviate teacher anxieties of losing control but to help these professionals and the children they love create social atmospheres of cooperation, contexts in which children and adults can learn together, play together, and build quality relationships.

In this chapter, we provide a brief overview of four basic theoretical models of human behavior and classroom management. These models are not the final word on working with children and adolescents with behavior problems. They are the fundamental concepts and approaches that professional educators have devised over the years. These are the four basic models:

1. Behavioral
2. Psychodynamic
3. Environmental
4. Constructivist

These four models differ in the way they define the sources or causes of human behavior. Also, they differ in the types of interventions they prescribe for teachers who are working with misbehaving children. Following each model summary, we list five essential questions that an educator using that single model would use in analyzing a behavior problem situation.

Prior to presenting the four models of behavior and intervention, we explain the social systems theory (or ecological theory) as a broader, more general framework for viewing the complex lives and behavior of students. Social systems theory allows us to envision students not only as individuals with characteristics, abilities, and personalities. It assumes that no individual truly lives and stands alone. We are all social beings that are influenced and defined by our networks of relationships with other persons. The social systems theory helps us to take into account the many social webs in which an individual lives, grows, and learns. It should be viewed as a background map on which the interventions of the four models of behavior and intervention may be plotted and carried out. We first present the social systems theory and then outline each of the four models of behavior and intervention.

SOCIAL SYSTEMS THEORY

Social systems theory teaches us that we never deal with just a child or a child's behavior. We always deal with a child in context, a person imbedded within and intimately connected to the surrounding physical and social world. Our efforts to aid or influence a child necessarily involve the contexts or ecologies in which that individual lives.

In social systems theory, child development is viewed as the continual adaptation or adjustment between an individual and the wide range of new and ever-changing social and physical environments. It is a progressive mutual accommodation that takes place throughout the life span between growing individuals and their life contexts. It is based on "the person's evolving conception of the ecological environment and his [or her] relationship to it, as well as the person's growing capacity to discover, sustain, or alter its properties" (Bronfenbrenner, 1979, p. 9).

Behavior is viewed as an expression of the dynamic relationship between the individual and the specific ecology in which the individual is situated or imbedded (Rhodes, 1967, 1970; Swap, 1978; Plas, 1986). Behavior occurs in a setting that includes a specific time, place, object "props," human relationships, and previously established patterns of behavior (Scott, 1980). By "previously established patterns of behavior," we mean those ways of behaving that are habitual to an individual, as he or she develops over time, and those past experiences that the individual brings to the setting in which the behavior is occurring.

Understanding the complexities of human behavior, therefore, requires more than the simple observation of an individual's behavior by one or two persons in a single setting, be that school classroom or home. It also requires an examination of the various systems of interaction of which an individual's behavior is only a part. In addition, to understand behavior one must take into account those aspects of the ecology or context *beyond* the immediate situation in which the individual is functioning that may impact on the behavior (Bronfenbrenner, 1979).

What is an ecology or ecological system? We'll draw an analogy from natural science to explain this. Take the example of a single plant. If we were to attempt to explain why that plant is healthy and thriving or why that plant is weak and dying, we might merely analyze the plant itself. We could look closely at the leaves, the roots, the stalk, and so on. To think in ecological terms involves expanding that analysis to look at the way the plant interacts with the various aspects of the natural surroundings. We might then look at questions about the amount of precipitation, the amount of shade and sunlight, the chemical composition of the soil, and the influences of other plants and animals. The single plant and the surrounding ecology are enmeshed, inseparable. One cannot speak of the plant without also speaking of the surrounding system, the ecology in which that plant lives and plays a part.

Moving a step further, we realize that this local ecology is intimately tied to larger ecologies. A patch of terrain is merely one section of a larger forest. That single forest is merely part of a vast, complex, worldwide ecological scheme that includes global weather patterns and astronomical phenomena.

Expanding our plant metaphor to children, we can easily see that most children live within a number of local ecological systems. Typically, we look at the family system, the classroom/school system, and the peer friendship network as the most important local ecologies in a child's life.

Systems theorists tend to talk about the importance of congruence. Congruence is the "match" or "goodness of fit" between the individual and an ecology. Thurman (1977) suggests that individuals whom persons judge to be "normal" are operating in an ecology that is congruent with that individual's actions. That individual's behavior is viewed as operating in harmony or in sync with the patterned norms of the social context. Thurman (1977) further maintains that when there is a lack of congruence, the individual is viewed as either deviant (being out of harmony with the norms) or incompetent (lacking the necessary behaviors). Congruence between the individual and the environment results in maximum competence and acceptance. According to Poplin and Stone (1992), an individual may be identified as having a disability when there is a mismatch between past and present experiences. The attitudes and behaviors that served the individual well in prior settings and situations are viewed as incongruent by persons within the new setting.

Bronfenbrenner suggests that the ecological contexts, or systems, in which an individual develops are nested, one inside the other, like a set of Russian dolls. He argues that the nested nature of the contexts is decisive in the individual's development as events take place within them. For example, he suggests that a child's ability to read may be related to the nature of the relationship between the child's home and school as well as the methods used in school to instruct reading.

Any individual change must be viewed within the context of the larger social and cultural systems (Riegel, 1975). As previously stated, these ecological systems are nested and dynamic. These contextual levels were originally called the ontogenic self (Kurdek, 1981), the microsystem, the mesosystem, the exosystem, and the macrosystem (Bronfenbrenner, 1979). For our purposes, we refer to these layered ecologies as the individual, interpersonal relationships, relationships between systems, group interactions, and society. We now define and explain each of these five nested ecologies.

The Individual

Kurdek (1981) suggests that though Bronfenbrenner's ecological contexts provide an essential recognition of the complexity of human development, using only those contexts fails to take into account the individual differences or variations that each individual brings to his or her primary interpersonal relationship settings. He argues for the inclusion of the ontogenic system, suggested by Tinbergen (1951), within the social systems perspective. We refer to this system as "the individual."

The individual can be said to consist of an ever-changing array of personal characteristics. Among these characteristics are the cognitive, affective, communicative, social, and physical competencies that the individual brings to the settings in which he or she is living. Each individual has personal means for coping with the environment, including personality attributes, skills, abilities, and competencies.

While social systems theory admits that the individual brings a set of personal characteristics to each social ecology, those characteristics are subject to the interpretation of those persons who inhabit a given ecological system. For example, we may say that a personal characteristic of one child is her high degree of social skills. Yet that child's social skillfulness does not rest mysteriously somewhere inside her physical body or psychic structure. Her social abilities are interpreted by those persons who interact with and relate to her. This may even result in varied interpretations of her social skill development. Perhaps the child's fourth-grade teacher finds her to be cooperative and kind while her soccer coach describes her as unruly and disruptive. This difference may mean that the child does behave differently in these two social contexts. It also may reflect a difference in interpretation between the teacher and the coach. In this sense, we can see that while an individual brings a set of personal characteristics to each social setting, those characteristics are evaluated or interpreted by other persons who share the social setting.

Interpersonal Relationships

Human social systems are like spiders' webs. Each line of the web is a single relationship in the ever-changing social network. Over time, patterns of personal interaction and communication give each web, each social system, its own particular quality. In the home, a network of relationships occurs, running like strings that connect all family members; parent and parent, parent and child, sibling and sibling. In the school, influential relationships occur between the child and teacher, as well as between the child and peers. Additionally, children (and adults, for that matter) often bundle themselves together into small groups, subsystems united by common interests and the bonds of friendship.

Relationships Between Systems

Relationships between systems may include the interrelations among home and school, home and service agency, home and neighborhood, and school and peer group. For example, students from minority cultural, ethnic, and linguistic groups may be challenged by the interrelationships between their home culture and the school culture and, as a consequence, be overrepresented as a group in special education. Parent-teacher collaboration and family-community service involvement are included within this system. Relationships between settings include consideration of transitions, or the movement of the individual between educational and employment settings.

Group Interaction

Group interactions describe the way that aspects of various systems relate to each other. For example, changes in a parent's workplace may affect the family system, producing new tensions or problems. This, in turn, may influence a child, bringing him to feel anxiety or fear. In this way, seemingly isolated ecologies interact and affect each other. These interacting systems may include a parent's workplace, a sibling's classroom, and the various components of a school system. Factors such as the availability of special education service programs, the goals of educational programs in the community, and the selection of school systemwide instructional materials and textbooks are examples of school-based group interactions.

Society

At the broadest level of social systems theory, we understand that major institutions, political activities, moral norms, and shifting philosophies occurring across society intertwine to impact the life of an individual. A child who is raised in late 20th-century America experiences a social world vastly different from a child raised in early 18th-century America or in late 20th-century Guatemala. The vast political, economic, and social world provides the context in which an individual life is formed and understood.

Daily, in a wide variety of settings and institutions, the persons and group of society are involved in the continuous making and remaking of cultural norms. These norms are sometimes ambiguous. Sometimes there are clear guidelines for human action and social interaction. The question asked and answered constantly as people go about their daily business is, What is right? Often the cultural norms that are enacted in public schools and other major institutions reflect the values and belief systems of dominant groups. Simultaneously, though, alternative norms are constructed by persons and groups that disagree with dominant and socially mandated ways.

In this societal mix of clarity, conflict, and uncertainty, most crucial to our topic of behavior management is the moral question, What is good or bad behavior? Since no timeless, universal standards of child behavior have been etched across the sky, determinations of what constitutes good and bad child behavior vary greatly. Certainly, in the midst of this ambiguity, a variety of social forces influence how parents and professionals view and evaluate the behavior of children. Ultimately, ethical questions are decided by individuals and groups within actual lived situations, the day-to-day sorting out of specific problems and possibilities. We all make such decisions.

IMPLICATIONS OF SOCIAL SYSTEMS THEORY FOR BEHAVIOR MANAGEMENT

If there is one concept we would like readers to gather from social systems theory, it is this: An individual is inextricably intertwined by way of human relationship with social networks both small and large. If the general goals of behavior management practices are to help children to both improve their behavior and take greater control over what they do, then social systems theory teaches us that there are many systemic points at which a concerned person may intervene to help a child or adolescent.

For example, imagine a six-year-old boy named Philip. Mrs. Sherman, his teacher, has struggled to help him improve his negative and disruptive behavior in his first-grade class. Philip tends to be easily frustrated and sometimes throws temper tantrums when he does not get what he wants. Without going into great detail, we can imagine many possible interventions occurring at many points in the various ecological levels. For the sake of this illustration, let's imagine that first-grade teacher initiating five specific interventions, each focusing on a different ecological level. Each intervention could possibly influence Philip's feelings and behavior in positive and negative ways.

1. *Individual.* Mrs. Sherman gradually teaches Philip what anger is, how it feels, how to notice when he is becoming angry, and how to manage his anger in less disruptive ways.
2. *Interpersonal relationships.* Mrs. Sherman plans a number of times each week when she or her classroom aide and Philip can spend personal time together enjoying each other and improving their relationship.
3. *Relationships between systems.* Mrs. Sherman talks extensively with Philip's mother about the problem, sharing ideas and concerns.
4. *Group interactions.* Mrs. Sherman arranges for Philip and his mother to meet with the guidance counselor to discuss ways to help Philip learn to manage his anger.

5. *Society.* Mrs. Sherman observes Philip closely to understand more fully when and why he actually becomes angered. She finds that he tends to want to keep objects likes toys and school supplies to himself. In fact, many of Mrs. Sherman's students do not like sharing with others. Mrs. Sherman feels that much of American society engages in a competition to own goods and property as an attempt to be fulfilled. She decides to attempt to teach her entire class to be more cooperative than competitive, more communal than selfish.

While a nonprofessional may not address the situation with such a multidimensional approach, this example provides a glimpse of how interventions may be implemented at many ecological levels.

In the following sections, we describe the primary models of behavior management. Because these models have been developed primarily for use by professionals who deal directly with children in local ecologies, these models tend to emphasize interventions aimed toward the inner rings of the ecological circles. Note how each model has its own way of conceptualizing a behavior problem and intervening toward improvement.

BEHAVIORAL MODEL

Harkening back to the work of behavioral science pioneers like Watson (1930/1970), Thorndike (1932), Wolpe (1973), Bandura (1969), and Skinner (1974), the behavioral model is concerned with the scientific modification of observable behaviors. This is accomplished through the precise alteration of stimuli, the influential aspects of an individual's immediate environment. Behaviorists hold that environmental variables all but dictate an individual's behavior. From the standpoint of the behavioral model, all behavior is conditioned by external stimuli. Those behaviors that are conditioned and exhibited by a person are controlled by the environmental stimuli that immediately surround the individual.

The source of specific behaviors can be found in the environmental stimuli that reward, fail to reward, or punish. In this sense, the person's many behaviors are literally viewed as "responses" occurring in relation to specific stimuli in the environment. Interventions designed to change behavior involve the careful study of the stimuli that promote or discourage a given behavior. Once the specific stimuli are identified, then those stimuli may be altered in order to increase or decrease the probability that the targeted behavior will occur. In short, a behavior is changed through the strategic modification of the environmental stimuli that influence that behavior. This usually involves the introduction of reinforcers according to the behavioral principles of reinforcement.

There are five basic principles of reinforcement that should be followed in order to increase a target behavior (desired behavior to be increased). First, reinforcement or reward must only be presented when the target behavior is exhibited. Reinforcement is only effective if it is specifically applied to the target behavior. Second, the reinforcer should be presented immediately after the target behavior is exhibited. If a time delay between the target behavior and the reward occurs, the likelihood that the behavior will be increased is greatly reduced. Third, initially, the target behavior must be reinforced every time it is exhibited. Fourth, once the target behavior has been increased to the desired level, then reinforcement should occur on an intermittent basis. The behavior is maintained at the achieved level by a schedule of inconsistent reinforcement. Lastly, tangible reinforcers should be accompanied by social reinforcers such as kind words and supportive smiles.

The primary three applications of this model in behavior management are *behavior modification* (Alberto & Troutman, 1995; Schloss & Smith, 1998; Van Houten & Axelrod, 1993), *functional analysis* (Iwata, 1994; Reichle & Wacker, 1993; Repp, 1994; Sugai & Tindal, 1993; Umbreit, 1996), and *pre-mod analysis* (Kaplan, 1995).

Behavior modification assumes that behaviors are exhibited by an individual primarily as a direct function of the *reinforcers* that occur immediately prior (antecedent) and/or immediately after (consequence) the behavior. Altering antecedents and consequences of behavior thereby modifies the behavior. The procedure for implementing a behavior modification plan involves the following steps:

1. Select the specific behavior to be changed.
2. Choose and introduce an influential reinforcer at the appropriate time.
3. Design and consistently present the reinforcer according to the behavioral principles of reinforcement.
4. Monitor the behavior over time and evaluate the effectiveness of the intervention.

Functional analysis is a technique of behavioral intervention that adds the complexity of context to the task of understanding the environmental variables (antecedent and consequent events) that support behaviors. Sugai and Tindal (1993) describe functional analysis as "a temporally based direct observation procedure designed to examine the relationship between behavior and setting variables" (p. 86). They further state that the purpose of an observation is threefold:

1. To collect a sample and a count of the behaviors exhibited by the individual
2. To document behavior chains, series of behaviors in which the occurrence of one behavior seems to trigger or promote the exhibition of the next behavior

3. Ultimately, to create an explanation for the individual's behavior that functionally links that behavior to events and behaviors occurring in temporal proximity (antecedents and consequences)

Based on this functional explanation, variables may be strategically altered and behavior may be changed.

Pre-mod analysis (Kaplan, 1995) adds emotional and cognitive dimensions to the strictly behavioral focus of functional analysis. While functional analysis assumes that a specific observable is "caused" or "promoted" by environmental stimuli occurring immediately before or after the behavior, pre-mod analysis looks closely at the emotional state and general personality of the child as possible explanations for behavior. Maybe the child feels anxious or upset. Maybe the child is impatient or impulsive. Maybe the child simply is unable to do the desired behavior. Short-term emotional states like anger or sadness and long-term emotional conditions or temperaments such as depression or impulsivity are viewed as good explanations for child behavior. Simply put, the individual child's feelings, thoughts, and personality are seen as influential and important.

The general goal of pre-mod analysis is to figure out what prerequisite skills (attitudes, social skills, feelings, knowledge) a child needs in order to be prepared to learn the desired behavior. From there, a series of interventions can be designed to fully prepare the student to learn the positive behavior. The general pre-mod procedure involves four steps:

1. Name the desired behavior. What should the student be doing?
2. Name the specific attitudes, knowledge, emotions, and skills that are prerequisites for this child exhibiting this behavior. Perhaps the child does not understand the behavior or the situations in which the behavior fits. Perhaps the child is too angry to actually do this behavior. Perhaps the desired behavior is far beyond this student's social skill development.
3. Evaluate the child's ability to learn this behavior based on your answers in step 2.
4. Based on the evaluation in step 3, design a series of interventions or lessons that will supply the child with the necessary prerequisite skills.

Five Essential Behavioral Questions

1. What is the *specific* behavior that is problematic?
2. Under what specific conditions does this behavior occur?
3. What are the antecedent and consequent conditions or events that tend to occur in conjunction with this behavior? (What happens before and after the behavior that might support or reinforce it?)

4. What is available that would be viewed as rewarding by the child or adolescent?
5. Who can systematically and consistently provide the rewards and how can this be arranged?

PSYCHODYNAMIC MODEL

While the behavioral model emphasizes the influential stimuli that exist physically *outside* a child, the psychodynamic model looks primarily *inside* the child. Based within a neo-Freudian understanding of individual psychology, this model views behavior as reflective of internal feelings and conflicts (Long & Morse, 1996; Redl & Wineman, 1951; Redl & Wineman, 1952). Wood and Long (1991) state this perspective clearly: "When working with children and youth . . . adults need to acknowledge, accept, understand, believe, and appreciate that emotions are the powerful, personal engines that drive or generate human behavior" (p. 158). Overwhelming feelings like anger, sadness, and confusion fuel overt behaviors. Often a child who is misbehaving is said to be "acting out" inner emotions, demonstrating how he or she feels at that moment. This demonstration is held to be, at least in part, unconscious or unintentional.

Psychodynamic interventions involve careful attention to the inner lives of children. Teachers employing the psychodynamic model believe in the daily priority of building trustful relationships with young persons in order to foster the development of self-esteem, personal insight, self-control, and social skills. While this adult-child or teacher-student relationship comes to the forefront when a social conflict or stressful incident occurs, the teacher realizes that much of the relational groundwork for working with children experiencing emotional distress occurs during "downtime," during the rather mundane moments when all seems calm and well. Buddying up to a student who is misbehaving is not the idea. Developing a form of intimacy and connection with students by talking, playing, and working together every day is the goal.

Additionally, the teacher utilizing a psychodynamic approach always remembers that he or she is not only dealing with overt behaviors. Observable behaviors, no matter how annoying or noxious, are the tip of the iceberg. Behaviors are pieces of surface evidence that teachers must interpret in order to understand the more pertinent emotions rumbling beneath. Working with a misbehaving child, in this model, involves attempting to influence not only how a child behaves. Lasting change is assumed to occur only from helping children to deal with the difficult feelings that stir beneath the behaviors.

The psychodynamic tradition advises teachers to help students develop themselves in two specific ways: *insight* and *trusting relationships*. A student with a highly developed sense of insight has a strong awareness of her feelings and how those feelings are acted out in her behaviors. Additionally, the student is aware of when and why painful or troubling feelings tend to arise for her, the kinds of situations, interactions, and social dynamics that bring about her own suffering. The practical side of insight occurs when students are able to isolate feelings from behaviors, realizing that while feelings of sadness and anger are very "normal" and acceptable, the translation of these feelings into behaviors is a matter of individual self-control. The student who becomes enraged and shouts obscenities at a peer can learn that the shouting behavior is not required by his feelings. Feeling the anger is probably unavoidable. But what one does, the actions one takes, while angry can be far more socially responsible than shouting obscenities.

Insight is not easy to come by. It involves a rationality and reflective capacity that are often unavailable to a student feeling overwhelmed and driven by intense emotions. This is where *trustful relationships* come into play. When a student is caught up in the midst of powerful feelings, it often takes the support of caring adults to help that student feel a capacity and desire for self-control. The nonjudgmental support of a teacher can be especially crucial given that most situations in which a student becomes engulfed in negative feelings occur within social conflicts. That is, children and adolescents often experience intense anger, sadness, guilt, and feelings of inadequacy during a conflict with other persons, during moments of strife and friction within relationships to people who matter to the student. The position of the teacher as a supportive, trusted adult can help to stabilize the emotional turmoil of difficult interpersonal conflicts and struggles, providing a sense of comfort and emotional safety, creating a soft place for a troubled student to land.

Behavior management strategies emerging from the psychodynamic tradition consist of *counseling techniques* and *behavior influence techniques*. We briefly describe each.

Counseling techniques involve dialogues that build trust between troubled or misbehaving children and caring adults. The general goals of these dialogues or discussions is to provide emotional support to children experiencing emotional pain while promoting self-understanding, social awareness, problem-solving skills, and self-control. As with all forms of counseling, these methods require nonjudgmental listening and supportive forms of interaction on the part of the adult. Three useful examples of counseling techniques are (1) *active listening*, (2) *responding with understanding*, and (3) *Life Space Intervention* (LSI).

George and Cristiani (1995) distinguish between the *active listening* necessary of a counselor in working with a troubled client and the typical forms of listening we use in social conversation. Within the give-and-take patterns of social conversation, we tend to listen while waiting to speak. The act of listening is somewhat shallow, occurring as one part of waiting to take the floor and speak. In contrast, *active listening* requires that a counselor or teacher set aside personal priorities and concerns to focus exclusively on the words, feelings, and perspective of the student who is speaking. This listening process occurs simultaneously on two levels. At the surface, the listener hears the words the student is expressing, the literal message. At a deeper level, the listener tunes in on the child's troubling predicament, the child's world at that moment, hearing and valuing that individual human experience. Although we all speak and listen every day, it is rare that someone is actually heard on this level and in this way. In psychodynamic theory, a teacher believes that such total listening is therapeutic for the student, providing a form of intimacy that supports the development of insight, moral concern, and healthy social relationships.

Responding with understanding, according to Egan (1975), takes active listening to the next step. Instead of evaluating the student's behavior or feelings, telling that student what is right or wrong about those actions and emotions, responding with understanding requires a teacher to reply to the student in a manner that demonstrates an understanding of the individual's predicament and perspective. This validates the student's worries, concerns, and perspective as real and worthwhile. Egan (1975) explains that when you respond with understanding, you do the following:

- you listen carefully to the other person's total communication—words, nonverbal messages, and voice-related cues;
- you try to identify the feelings the person is expressing and the experiences and behaviors that give rise to these feelings;
- you try to communicate to this person an understanding of what he or she seems to be feeling and the sources of these feelings;
- you respond not by evaluating what he or she has to say but by showing your understanding of the other person's world from that person's point of view. (p. 137)

The goal of this form of listening and response is to help the student know and feel that he or she is understood. This supports and comforts the student, thereby greatly increasing the individual's ability in that moment to look closely and responsibly at the problem at hand. The individual is empowered by support and relationship.

Life Space Intervention (LSI) is a fairly complex counseling process that utilizes both active listening and responding with understanding. We'll briefly summarize this process here, but we recommend that interested readers consult Wood and Long (1991) for a more detailed explanation.

LSI is on-the-spot counseling that emphasizes both the feelings that underlie behavior and a direct, problem-solving approach to constructively addressing a current situation. Typically, an LSI occurs immediately after a problem event or behavior incident. The adult gently calms the upset child and then guides that child through a careful and honest reconstruction of the entire incident. The teacher asks questions that help the child to reconstruct an incident narrative, the precise sequence of events prior to and including the incident itself. This process brings the student into confrontation with the actual events, what others did, and what he or she did. No blame is cast in this reconstruction. The initial goal is simply accuracy. Once the events have been set forth in full view of the teacher and student, then the teacher can encourage the student to locate the central issue of the matter, the primary conflict or misunderstanding that brought about the incident.

When both the teacher and the student can agree on the central issue or problem, then the teacher can support the student in accepting responsibility (not blame) for his portion of the problem. This approach assumes that all problems between persons are social and, therefore, that responsibility typically is spread across participants. Thus, sometimes the teacher may need to accept some responsible role in creating or perpetuating the problem.

With the problem identified and some degree of responsibility accepted, the student is prepared to work with the teacher to figure out how to solve or alleviate this situation. Perhaps some amends might be made, apologies offered. Perhaps there is a way to avoid such a problem in the future. Perhaps the student needs to develop specific social skills to do better next time. All these options are discussed in the problem-solving portion of the LSI. The LSI is completed with this practical discussion of what to do now, emphasizing the child's personal responsibility and self-control as an active problem solver.

While most psychodynamic interventions attempt to address the feelings that stir beneath behaviors, Redl and Wineman (1952) have offered twelve *behavior influence techniques* that deal explicitly with "surface" behaviors. These surface management techniques were developed in recognition of the fact that classroom teachers simply do not have time to conduct counseling sessions for every minor behavior problem that pops up. The twelve techniques are as follows:

1. Planned ignoring—ignoring minor, annoying behaviors that children do to gain attention
2. Signal interference—nonverbal ways that adults communicate to children that behavior is acceptable or unacceptable (e.g., a sharp look, clearing the throat, thumbs up, a nod and smile)
3. Proximity control—standing closer to a misbehaving child in order to gently assert adult authority
4. Interest boosting—breaking the sometimes dull routine of school tasks by either reorganizing a student's work or by offering supportive and encouraging words that reinvigorate a child's desire to complete the tasks
5. Tension reduction through humor—be fun and funny to increase joy and decrease anxiety
6. Hurdle helping—providing needed academic and emotional support to a child who struggles in difficult tasks

7. Program restructuring—setting aside or recasting a specific activity that is not holding the students' interest and attention
8. Support from routine—using daily routines and rituals to create comfort and emotional security
9. Direct appeal—clearly stating what is going wrong and entreating a student's sense of fairness by asking for a change in behavior
10. Removal of seductive objects—withdrawing objects that sway the child's interest away from the task at hand
11. Antiseptic bouncing—removing an upset and disruptive student from the group or classroom in order to help the child calm down, gain control, and start fresh
12. Physical restraint—(in accordance with professional codes of ethics and local district policies) asserting safe physical control over a child whose behavior has become dangerous to self and/or others.

Five Essential Psychodynamic Questions

1. What difficult feelings is the child or adolescent experiencing (anger, sadness, frustration) when she or he misbehaves?
2. Why is the child or adolescent feeling this? (What is going on at the moment or in the child or adolescent's life that stirs these feelings?)
3. Is there a way to arrange for the child or adolescent to move away from the situation and cool down at the time these difficult feelings are rising up?
4. Is there a way to arrange for an adult that the child or adolescent views as caring and trustworthy to provide support and talk privately with the child or adolescent about these difficult feelings when these feelings occur?
5. Is there a way to increase the number and quality of trusting, caring relationships with adults in this individual's life?

ENVIRONMENTAL MODEL

The environmental model (e.g. Hobbes, 1966; Rhodes & Paul, 1978; Swap, 1978) focuses on the development of specific aspects of a child's immediate environments (home, school, neighborhood) that provide structure, support, vitality, and regularity. To some extent, what a person does (behavior) is inseparable from context. For example, imagine a child (or an adult!) waking up each morning in a different bed. The entire house has been rearranged. Imagine further that the events of the day are completely unplanned. There is no continuity between one day and the next. The comfort of having some idea of what to expect is completely absent. Living within such an environmental context that offers no structure and consistency would be emotionally difficult for most people. On the other hand, a few individuals would find such a lifestyle fascinating and enjoyable.

Of course, consistency can be overwhelming and stifling. Imagine a daily setting in which a regime of detailed routines is the master of all human activities. At 6:02 A.M., a 3-second bell sounds. There are 9 minutes to eat breakfast, the same menu of cornflakes, milk, and slice of dry, wheat toast served everyday. At 6:11, the breakfast dishes must be placed in the sink. The cereal bowl goes in first. This is followed by the toast plate, topped by the spoon, and so on. At this prison-like extreme of order and regimentation, the living environment is humanly empty and even maddening.

The environmental model emphasizes the way the contexts in which a person lives greatly influences that person's behavior. There is no absolute formula for designing healthy contexts in which to live and learn. Individuals vary too greatly in demeanor and tastes for such certainty. Instead, the key is in fashioning contexts that match the personality and needs of the individual child. To this end, the environmental model focuses on the contributions of three specific areas of environmental organization to the behavior of children: time, physical space, and patterns of human interaction. We briefly discuss each of these three areas of environmental management. Each area consists as a list of questions to help adults consider the way environmental details and arrangements foster desirable and undesirable behavior.

Time

The primary question to consider is, Are the activities of the day (week, month, year) organized in such a way as to promote emotional comfort, cooperative behavior, and personal fulfillment?

Additional questions that are helpful in analyzing time more carefully include the following:

- Is the day scheduled too tightly (over-ordered) or too loosely (under-ordered) for this child?
- Does the daily schedule include a balance of meaningful routines and opportunities for improvisation?
- Is the schedule clear and understandable to the child?
- What role does the child play in the planning of activities?
- Are there specific aspects of the day in which behavior problems are more likely?
- How can the daily activities be redesigned to avoid or alter these trouble spots?

Physical Space

The primary question to consider is, Are physical objects (such as chairs, tables, desks, lighting, and other materials) arranged in such a way as to promote bodily comfort, emotional ease, concentration to task, constructive communication, and positive relationships with others?

Additional questions that are helpful in analyzing physical space more carefully include the following:

- Does the physical space, including furniture, lighting, flooring, and materials, support the successful completion of the desired activities?
- Is the room or area overcrowded? Too noisy? Unattractive?
- Are the instructional or recreational materials adequate to support the tasks?
- Do the children need help in organizing and using their own materials?
- Do the children have adequate personal space for themselves and their belongings?

Patterns of Human Interaction

Patterns of human interaction within groups (families, classroom groups) are oft-repeated sequences of behaviors that often are maintained within habits and rules. Individuals and groups have habits, typical patterns of behavior that are repeated each day. To some extent, what an individual or group did yesterday is likely to be recreated today.

Rules often govern what happens. We should think of two different types of rules, explicit and implicit, each very powerful in explaining the behavior of individuals within group contexts. Explicit rules are the official rules, those that teachers post on the wall or schools write in schoolwide disciplinary policy handbooks. Explicit rules are often created and enforced by authority figures like parents and teachers to influence the behavior of children. Implicit rules are the informal or unofficial rules that govern and order interactions within the group. These are the cultural codes, practices, and manners that people tend to simply assume. For instance, the social practice of saying "excuse me" under specific types of situations is an implicit rule that is often (but not always) enacted. In the school classroom, a variety of traditional student social practices would be considered implicit rules, such as addressing the teacher as Mrs., Mr., or Miss; asking permission before going to the rest room; storing personal materials in one's own desk or locker; and using lower volume voice tones in the library than in the gymnasium.

Additionally, we should realize that students themselves create and maintain a wide variety of implicit rules or social codes that influence and order their interactions and relationships. These micro-level behavioral codes involve various student roles (popular student, brainy student, class clown, etc.), friendship clusters, and the power relations amongst and between. Social patterns concerning who interacts with whom, the style and content of those interactions, norms of communication and behavior, as well as activities of rejection, violation, and acceptance occur within the ever-flexing realm of implicit social rules. Even the way that explicit rules are handled (upheld, modified, transgressed) depends on the implicit rules of the classroom and school.

Patterns of behavior within a group can often be changed by altering the rules, explicit and implicit, that govern behavior. The primary question in regard to patterns of human interaction to consider is, How do the current habits and rules of the group promote or not promote the desired behaviors (cooperation, attention to task, etc.)?

Additional questions that are helpful in analyzing patterns of human interaction more carefully include the following:

- Are there clear procedures and norms for the many types of interaction? For answering questions? For talking to peers? For working together in small groups?
- Are the rules of classroom behavior clear to all?
- Are the rules conducive to respect and cooperation?
- Are there "unwritten" rules that take precedence over the overt rules?
- If so, do these "unwritten" rules support positive behavior and respectful interactions?
- Are both written and "unwritten" rules respectful of the diversity of ethnic, cultural, and gender norms of belief and behavior?
- Is there sufficient opportunity for the children to seek meaningful changes in habits or norms that do not serve them?

Five Essential Environmental Questions

1. For each of the recent instances of misbehavior or conflict, describe the physical setting, time of day, activity, and participants. (Keeping observational field notes for a number of days can help with this task.)
2. Do you notice any repeated patterns in regard to question 1?
3. Does the individual or group experiencing the behavior problems have any discomfort with the setting, time schedule, activity, or participants? (Ask!)
4. If you do notice patterns in how certain settings, times of day, activities, or participants provoke or promote the problematic behavior, what changes can reasonably be made?

5. What is your own (teacher's) role as a powerful element of the social context in contributing to or improving upon this problem situation? (This can be a tough one.)

CONSTRUCTIVIST MODEL

Derived from the works of scholars like Piaget (1954, 1970) and Bruner (1962, 1986, 1996), constructivism operates under the assumption that children are not passive receptacles of information but active constructors of personal and social meaning. Within their thoughts, feelings, words, and actions, children continuously create what is meaningful, valuable, and important to them. In this sense, children are constantly constructing personal knowledge about themselves and the world. This knowledge concerns personal identity, relationships with important others, cultural norms, and moral stances. From this perspective, we must keep in mind that even behavior we deem "inappropriate" is meaningful and important in some way to the child or children who do the behavior.

In addition to the personal meaningfulness of constructed knowledge, constructivism draws from the field of cultural anthropology in holding that much of what an individual "knows" and "believes" is shared with other persons (Bruner, 1996). In this sense, one's words and ideas are not merely individual inventions. They are shared cultural ways of understanding and thinking about human living. Persons of a common culture or subculture (like a classroom or school) tend to borrow ideas, beliefs, and words from each other. Meaningful and important values concerning how a person should behave in specific types of situations tend to be shared among groups of persons. Changes in those values and cultural codes occur on both the individual and the larger group level.

Additionally, drawing from the work of resistance theorists (Foley, 1990; MacLeod, 1995; McLaren, 1993; Willis, 1977), constructivists believe that cultural life is often filled with conflict and political strife. What counts as important and meaningful is not predetermined and fixed for all time. It is the subject of continuous struggle between various groups. Often these subcultural groups occur on the basis of social class, race, gender, sexual orientation, or other distinctions. Some dominant groups tend to set the values and other less dominant groups tend to resist or contest those values. This conflict occurs not only in the community but also in the public schools. Drawing from the resistance theory knowledge base, constructivists realize that determining "the right behavior" or "the right thing to do" in a given situation is not a simple matter. Morally right behavior is an area of struggle within society and within schools among a variety of participants who disagree about basic values and ways of life.

Based on the theoretical stances stated above, the constructivist model emphasizes the development of individual moral autonomy (Fields & Tarlow, 1996), the importance of caring for others (Henderson, 1996), and the building of supportive and diverse communities (Kohn, 1996).

Moral Autonomy

Moral autonomy is an individual's ongoing sense of self as a responsible moral agent, a concerned evaluator of what is good and what is bad in each life situation. A child with a well-developed moral autonomy is exploratory, continuously questioning herself about what is good. This questioning occurs not out of confusion but out of a pervasive feeling of concern for the well-being of self and others.

Fields and Tarlow (1996) present three general strategies designed to support the development of moral autonomy. These are for use when teachers deal directly with a student:

1. *Reciprocal respect.* Teachers often do not realize when they speak to children in harsh and cruel ways. We must remember that a child who is treated with respect will often reciprocate with respectful, cooperative behavior. Respect is something that teachers must earn. It is not something that can be demanded. Only fearful compliance can be demanded. Respect is earned by giving respect and by seeking similar dignified treatment in return.

2. *Related consequences.* If consequences (or punishments) are logically related to the misbehavior, then the student is more likely to learn a desirable lesson. The idea is that consequences should not simply inflict emotional suffering on the misbehaving child under the simplistic notion that bad behavior must be punished. Consequences should improve the problem situation itself and prepare a student for future moral decision making. For example, a child who steals can provide restitution of the stolen object. A child who makes a mess can clean it up. If a child physically or emotionally harms another person, the child can take action to reduce the victim's pain or discomfort. Obviously, this model of creating consequences for misbehavior does not involve preset, mandatory punishments. The use of related consequences requires flexibility so that the punishment can fit logically with the specific misbehavior. Additionally, this approach often works best when consequences are actually negotiated between the student and teacher. This helps the student take responsibility for the misbehavior and the acts of restitution and resolution.

3. *Effective communication.* Here is where the constructivists appreciate and appropriate the counseling techniques of the psychodynamic model. Open communication, free of judgments and shaming, involves active listening and collaborative problem solving. Active listening means listening wholeheartedly without offering advice or direction. Collaborative problem solving means that solutions are not merely dictated by adults but are negotiated in good faith between child and adult.

Caring

After visiting many classrooms for students with severe emotional and behavioral difficulties, Morse (1994) finally realized the one characteristic shared by all gifted teachers. The students in these teachers' classrooms were fully convinced that their teachers were concerned about their well-being. Regardless of teaching techniques or tactics, the students knew completely that this teacher cared.

The act of caring for others is not viewed by the constructivist model as an individual behavior or a series of skills. A person who cares for others does not learn to do so single-handedly. Caring is always an aspect of relationship (Noddings, 1984; 1992). It is shared between two persons or among an intimately connected group such as a family or class of students. Caring is a quality of ethical, human connection in which each person is genuinely invested in the well-being of the other(s).

Central to this concept of an ethical, valuing relationship is a deep concern with the possibilities for the misuse of power within relationships between adults and children. A misuse of power violates what caring is all about. Henderson (1996) explains that teachers too often utilize "power over" students, a top-down form of authoritarian control that relies on the coercive influence of rewards, punishments, and threats. Coercion may produce short-term compliance, but it also creates children who are powerless and teacher-student relationships characterized by distance and lack of empathy. The concept of "power with" emphasizes the need for adult authority figures to share decision making with children. Children are invited into an ongoing and open dialogue with adults to make decisions concerning what is best for all members of the class or group. Such involvement in the building of an interdependent community allows children to feel responsible for themselves and their community.

Community Building

Both Henderson (1996) and Kohn (1996) emphasize the need for schools to build democratic communities of social cohesion that value the many forms of human diversity. Henderson (1996) presents a complete community-building protocol for classroom teachers to build a supportive unit among their students. While this protocol is too long to summarize here, we can point out some highlights of the approach. Community cannot be mandated by way of rules. It can be fostered gradually by a teacher who feels comfortable sharing power and responsibility.

The teacher who builds community reflects repeatedly on both the distribution of power and the quality of interactions within the social group. The goal is to lead a group of students to become caring equals, collaborators personally involved in co-constructing a learning community. Henderson emphasizes that teachers can be strategic and purposeful actors in

MacLeod, J. (1995). *Ain't no makin' it.* Boulder, CO: Westview Press.

McLaren, P. (1993). *Schooling as a ritual performance.* New York: Routledge.

Morse, W. C. (1994). The role of caring in teaching children with behavior problems. *Contemporary Education, 65*(3), 132–136.

Noddings, N. (1984). *Caring, a feminine approach to ethics and moral education.* Berkeley: University of California Press.

Noddings, N. (1992). *The challenge to care in schools: An alternative approach to education.* New York: Teachers College Press.

Piaget, J. (1954). *The construction of reality in the child.* New York: Basic Books.

Piaget, J. (1970). *The child's conception of physical causality.* London: Routledge & Kegan Paul.

Plas, J. M. (1986). *Systems psychology in the schools.* Elmsford, NY: Pergamon Books.

Poplin, M. S., & Stone, S. (1992). Paradigm shifts in instructional strategies. In W. Stainback & S. Stainback (Eds.), *Controversial issues confronting special education.* Boston: Allyn & Bacon.

Redl, F., & Wineman, D. (1951). *Children who hate: The disorganization and breakdown of behavior controls.* New York: Free Press.

Redl, F., & Wineman, D. (1952). *Controls from within: Techniques for the treatment of the aggressive child.* Glencoe, IL: Free Press.

Reichle, J., & Wacker, D. (1993). *Communicative alternatives to challenging behavior: Integrating functional assessment and interventional strategies.* Baltimore: Brookes.

Repp, A. (1994). Comments on functional analysis procedures for school-based behavior problems. *Journal of Applied Behavior Analysis, 27*(2), 409–411.

Riegel, K. F. (1975). Toward a dialectical theory of development. *Human Development, 18,* 50–64.

Rhodes, W. C. (1967). The disturbing child: A problem of ecological management. *Exceptional Children, 33,* 449–455.

Rhodes, W. C. (1970). A community participation analysis of emotional disturbance. *Exceptional Children, 36,* 309–314.

Rhodes, W. C., & Paul, J. L. (1978). *Emotionally disturbed and deviant children: New views and approaches.* Upper Saddle River, NJ: Prentice Hall.

Schloss, P. J., & Smith, M. A. (1998). *Applied behavior analysis in the classroom.* Boston: Allyn & Bacon.

Scott, M. (1980). Ecological theory and methods of research in special education. *Journal of Special Education, 4,* 279–294.

Skinner, B. F. (1974). *About behaviorism.* New York: Knopf.

Sugai, G. M., & Tindal, G. A. (1993). *Effective school consultation: An interactive approach.* Pacific Grove, CA: Brooks/Cole.

Swap, S. M. (1978). The ecological model of emotional disturbance in children: A status report and proposed synthesis. *Behavioral Disorders, 3*(3), 186–196.

Thorndike, E. L. (1932). *The fundamentals of learning.* New York: Teachers College Press.

Thurman, E. D., & Marshall, M. J. (1977). Clinical evaluation and coordination of services: An ecological model. *Exceptional Children, 44,* 16–22.

Tinbergen, N. (1951). *The study of instinct.* London: Oxford University Press.

Umbreit, J. (1996). Functional analysis of disruptive behavior in an inclusive classroom. *Journal of Early Intervention, 20*(1), 18–29.

Van Houten, R., & Axelrod, S. (1993). *Behavior analysis and treatment.* New York: Plenum Press.

Watson, J. B. (1930/1970). *Behaviorism.* New York: W. W. Norton.

Willis, P. (1977). *Learning to labour.* Farnborough, England: Saxon House.

Wolpe, J. (1973). *The practice of behavior therapy.* New York: Pergamon Press.

Wood, M. M., & Long, N. J. (1991). *Life Space Intervention.* Austin, TX: Pro-Ed.

CHAPTER TWO

How to Analyze a Case

In this chapter we present a format for case analysis that may be applied to the cases throughout the remainder of the book. This format includes both immediate intervention and long-term intervention. Immediate intervention is on-the-spot action taken to reduce a dangerous or threatening situation. Long-term intervention involves careful planning and action designed to help a child or group improve behavior and relationships. Both types of intervention are salient for classroom teachers concerned with behavior problems at school and professionals who consult with parents and community members who care for children in nonschool settings.

Following the presentation of the case analysis format, we demonstrate the format in application to a behavior problem case. Our purpose is to provide a concrete example of how a case may be analyzed in order to produce a number of possible effective interventions.

Critical Reflection as Thoughtful Case Analysis

Cases attempt to imitate the complexities of real life by refusing to submit to simplistic treatments. While one can respond to complicated, multidimensional cases or real-life situations with quick, knee-jerk judgments, we believe that good teaching and effective behavior management require a more thoughtful process called "critical reflection." This means thinking beyond one's immediate, armchair appraisal of a situation to consider alternative explanations that recast the scenario from different points of view. The teacher or professional who demonstrates critical reflection is able to view a situation from various perspectives and through a number of different theoretical lenses. Critical reflection combines a mental flexibility with a moral concern for the well-being of all persons involved.

Harrington, Quinn-Leering, and Hodson (1996) borrow heavily from the work of philosopher John Dewey in defining critical reflection according to three distinct elements: *open-mindedness*, *responsibility*, and *wholeheartedness*. Each of these elements call upon an educator to analyze situations in a way that generally goes beyond egocentrism, moving out from the confined logic of one's own standpoint to understanding broader dimensions and alternative ways of understanding. The impetus to move beyond one's own logic, beyond the comfort of one's usual way of seeing things, arises from the assumption that one's own perspective is inevitably limited and faulty. Continuous expansion of this perspective and reconsideration of personal beliefs about one's students will enable a teacher to broaden his or her array of useful techniques and skills.

Open-mindedness is the ability and willingness to recognize and value the validity of other perspectives beyond one's own, to realize that one's own way of viewing or describing a situation is not necessarily the best. This is a matter of remaining fallible and flexible, of attempting to be helpful instead of trying to be right. Seeing beyond the scope of one's usual way of viewing students and behavior problems is a difficult matter. We all tend not to notice our own blind spots, to remain unaware of what we are missing, as we move through each day within the limitations of our personal ideologies and understandings. Cultivating open-mindedness often involves developing a vulnerability to new and even "strange" ideas.

Responsibility is the ability and willingness to examine the possible ethical and political consequences of one's choices, to realize that whatever one chooses to do will impact the lives of others in foreseen and unforeseen ways. This is a matter of fully owning the many positive and negative ways your actions might influence the lives of others, regardless of how things turn out. Blaming a student for not responding to a teacher's intervention is the direct opposite of taking responsibility. Students have no obligation to behave as we predict they will. Accepting one's limitations and fallibility as a professional demonstrates responsibility.

Wholeheartedness is the ability and willingness to identify the limitations of one's own reasoning and assumptions when making a decision, to understand the partial nature of any description of a situation, and to appreciate the biases and values that inhabit one's own way of defining a problem and offering solutions. This is a matter of knowing yourself, your unique perspective, and where you are coming from as you look at human problem situations. A teacher can develop this kind of self-knowledge through examination of one's personal biography, analyzing how one's current way of viewing students and teaching are the culmination of years of personal experience (Danforth, 1997).

Ideally, these three aspects of critical reflection will be evidenced in the way one defines problems, designs immediate and long-term interventions, and evaluates the results of interventions. For university instructors using this book as part of a course in classroom or behavior management, we provide an evaluation rubric that incorporates critical reflection and other pertinent performance criteria (see table). This rubric is designed for the evaluation of an individual student's written case analysis. It could also be easily used for the evaluation of oral analyses of cases.

Evaluation Component	Good	Acceptable	Poor
Problem Identification	Clearly and fully describes problems in (a) multiple useful ways or (b) the most useful way, while remaining true to the facts of the case	Adequately describes problems in (a) multiple useful ways or (b) the most useful way, while remaining true to the facts of the case	Fails to describe problems in (a) multiple useful ways or (b) the most useful way, while remaining true to the facts of the case
Critical Reflection*	Fully demonstrates open-mindedness, responsibility, and wholeheartedness*	Demonstrates an adequate degree of open-mindedness, responsibility, and wholeheartedness*	Fails to demonstrate open-mindedness, responsibility, and wholeheartedness*
Use of Theoretical Concepts and Vocabulary	Fully utilizes the theory(ies) of behavior management that are suitable and useful for the particular case	Adequately utilizes the theory(ies) of behavior management that are suitable and useful for the particular case	Fails to utilize the theory(ies) of behavior management that are suitable and useful for the particular case
Plan of Action	Clearly and fully describes useful, logically reasonable short- and long-term interventions as necessitated by the case	Adequately describes useful, logically reasonable short- and long-term interventions as necessitated by the case	Fails to describe useful, logically reasonable short- and long-term interventions as necessitated by the case
Evaluation of Plan of Action	Provides ample evidence that most drawbacks or limitations of short- and long-term interventions have been considered	Provides some evidence that most drawbacks or limitations of short- and long-term interventions have been considered	Provides no evidence that most drawbacks or limitations of short- and long-term interventions have been considered
Organization, Presentation, and Grammar	Writing is well-organized, logically presented, and grammatically correct	Writing is adequate in regard to organization, logical presentation, and grammatical correctness	Writing is inadequate in regard to organization, logical presentation, and grammatical correctness

Evaluation Rubric for Students' Written Analyses of Cases

Source: From an unpublished evaluative rubric graciously supplied by Rita Silverman of Pace University.

*From "Written Case Analyses and Critical Reflection" by H. L. Harrington, Quinn-Leering, and L. Hodson, 1996, *Teaching and Teacher Education, 12*(1), 25–37.

Immediate Intervention

A toy flies across the room. A hand reaches out and grabs a clump of hair. Shouts and anger and threats ring out. A fist flies and blood is drawn. It can all happen so fast.

Often teachers must react quickly to problem situations. A conflict between children or with an individual's behavior can escalate to levels that threaten safety and demand immediate action. Such intervention does not involve systems of observation and careful planning. There is no time to sit down with a colleague or a friend and design a plan of action.

What caring adults can do is be prepared in advance. Preparation primarily involves anticipation, having a clear mental picture of what you can do if a problem arises. The purpose of this section is to provide an outline of priorities and immediate actions that professionals can take to diffuse a dangerous or threatening situation.

There are three basic goals of immediate intervention. We list them here in order of priority:

1. Ensure physical safety.
2. Attend to the emotional well-being of those most centrally involved.
3. Return the setting to a state of order and peace.

Ensuring Physical Safety

The physical safety of both the misbehaving child(ren) and others is the greatest priority. Intervention for this purpose may involve the use of physical means, language (talking to the threatening child and others), and removal of children from the area. The goal is to eliminate quickly and safely the possibility of violence and harm to any person. This requires a cool head, an even voice tone, and decisive action. Remember that it is possible that an intervention will actually further exacerbate the problem, increasing the danger to all.

For example, a 7-year-old boy holding a pair of scissors over his head chases a peer. Diffusing the danger of the situation requires that the child either give up the scissors or at least stop brandishing them as a weapon. Simple words of direction may do the trick. Yet, simply telling an angry child to hand over the scissors may have no impact. Physically grasping the boy's arm and pulling the scissors from his hand may be necessary. Also, adults may need to move the boy to another room or area. A word of warning: Professionals who engage in any interventions utilizing physical force should consult codes of professional ethics and school district or agency guidelines concerning such activity. Physically subduing children who are acting out should not be taken lightly.

Obviously, there are many risks to the adult and child in such situations. Additionally, we must realize that dealing with a 7-year-old boy waving a pair of scissors and a 15-year-old armed with a knife are not the same thing. Any professional must be aware of her or his own physical ability. Some adults can easily catch a running 7-year-old and snatch away the scissors. Some adults may not be able to handle this athletic feat.

We must always remember that standing up physically to an angry, possibly violent child or adolescent is a serious undertaking. An adult attempting to physically subdue a violent child should proceed with great caution in order to avoid injuring not only oneself but also the child and others in the vicinity. When in doubt (and doubt is well advised in a dangerous situation), we recommend that the room or area be cleared of peers and adults. This action removes possible targets of violent action. Often it is better to remove possible victims rather than to directly take on the threatening individual. Additionally, for professionals who deal with violent and threatening situations regularly, we recommend a complete training course in crisis intervention.

Attending to Emotional Well-Being

Once the danger has been successfully eliminated, emotions continue to run full and fast. Hearts are pounding, hands are sweating. All involved, including the misbehaving child or children, need to deal with the intense feelings that accompany such an incident. If feelings are ignored, other problems and conflicts are likely to follow.

Wood and Long (1991) describe this process as providing emotional first aid. In a sense, the emotions of all involved have been laid bare, opened like a wound. Immediate attention is required in order to support and vent intense feelings and confirm that a state of safety and peace has been restored. Simply put, this process involves talking to children about their feelings in a supportive manner. Adults need to listen and value the words of children, assure them that their feelings are real and normal. Finally, adults must provide reassurance that all is well. As Wood and Long (1991, p. 162) say, the general message is that "it's OK to feel like this; it will get better."

Returning Order and Peace

Of course, intervening to eliminate the physical danger and addressing the intense emotions of all involved means little if the situation is not quickly guided back to a comfortable state of order and peace. Once emotions have been discussed and persons feel able to return to their typical activities, it is important to return to business as usual. We do not wish to encourage any form of denial in which everyone pretends that things are okay when no one actually feels safe and comfortable. The order and peace of our usual habits cannot be forced or artificially contrived. Additionally, be aware that not all individuals restore themselves to calm and the usual business at the same speed. In a school classroom, some students may feel ready to return to their academic work within minutes after a serious upheaval. Others, particularly those most involved in the incident, may take substantially more time to feel calm and able to reengage in the activities of the day.

LONG-TERM INTERVENTION

If a single incident of misbehavior occurred, strategies of behavior management would hardly be necessary. Behavior management interventions are designed to create and maintain change in ongoing patterns of negative behavior. We call these long-term interventions because, unlike immediate interventions, they are designed and implemented for the purposes of promoting lasting, positive change in patterns of individual and/or group behavior.

Exactly what does and does not constitute a behavior problem requiring long-term intervention can be the subject of much debate. Behavior that one person finds intolerable and even immoral is deemed by another to be completely acceptable. We encourage professionals and parents to discuss these matters with trusted and knowledgeable colleagues and friends. There are no absolutes when deciding whether to intervene or allow behavior to continue. To some extent, we can understand that time and nonintervention tend to change some patterns of behavior and emotion eventually. The depressed person who does not seek treatment often weathers the storm and the depression lifts. A young child who spits at his siblings will probably, in time, stop spitting. How long these changes will take without intervention is not known. Understanding this, any teacher thinking of implementing a long-term intervention must seriously consider the well-being of the child and all persons connected to that child by way of interaction and relationship. Whether to intervene and how to intervene are ultimately moral choices.

If the decision is made to construct and carry out a long-term intervention, there are five general steps that guide one from analysis to action. We present these steps as basic guidelines, noting that they fit some models of intervention better than others. For instance, a highly rational step-by-step scheme works very nicely within a behavioral approach. In contrast, the psychodynamic and constructivist models tend to be more free flowing and contextual, often combining the steps listed below into a seamless course of action. These are the five steps:

1. Assessing the problem
2. Formulating objectives of intervention

3. Planning an effective intervention
4. Implementing the intervention
5. Evaluating the results

Additionally, as we emphasized in the first chapter discussion of social systems theory, interventions can occur at multiple ecological levels. Many professional programs of intervention simultaneously utilize strategies at different ecological levels.

Assessing the Problem

What's the problem here? How one defines a problem will logically influence how one intervenes. The various models of behavior management come into play at this point. Each model views the problem in a different light.

The behavioral model sees the source of the problem in the environmental stimulus or stimuli that reward or promote an individual's negative behavior. Often, though, the concern is not in finding the stimulus that encourages the problem. Instead, the focus is on finding a stimulus that can be introduced to decrease the negative behavior or increase a positive behavior. Simply, what reward program will modify the behavior? Systematic observations may be recorded in order to count the frequency of the target behavior before, during, and after the intervention period.

The psychodynamic model views a behavior problem as an outward symptom of unresolved, underlying feelings. The problem is primarily the uncomfortable and influential feelings that rumble beneath the surface. Assessment of the situation is twofold: First, professionals utilize insight to interpret these underlying emotions and the relational conflicts that feed the emotions; second, professionals talk with the child or children to ascertain their understanding of the emotions that fuel their behavior.

The environmental model looks to the way the environmental organization contributes to the behavior of children. How does the daily schedule of activities influence behavior? How do aspects of the physical environment encourage or discourage certain behaviors? What are the usual patterns of human interaction, and how do they support or fail to support certain behaviors?

The constructivist model looks at the quality of relationships between child and important others, with a noted emphasis on respectfulness, community, and caring. Of concern within this problem definition are inequalities and conflicts that exist between various participants and the way those inequalities create resentment and negative behavior.

No matter which model one chooses to work in and through, a clear formulation of the problem is crucial. You may find out later that your assessment was misguided or inaccurate. Remember that behavior management involves trial and error. Nonetheless, a teacher must define the problem in order to develop an intervention plan.

Formulating Objectives of Intervention

Now that you have defined the problem, a new question arises: What change(s) do you want to accomplish through the intervention? This change could take many forms. You could identify a specific behavior that you will try to modify. You may attempt to help a child deal with uncomfortable and difficult feelings. You may try to influence and improve patterns of relationship involving a child or a group. You may attempt to reorganize the daily schedule of activities to promote certain positive changes in one or more children.

As a general rule, it is best to seek relatively modest forms of change. Grandiose plans to refashion groups and individuals into completely new persons often fail miserably. Set simple and realistic goals. Often a plan that begins with the most accessible changes is best.

One should have a clear understanding of the goals or objectives of the intervention. This clarity will help you devise the intervention plan. Additionally, after the intervention has been implemented, you can compare the results to your original intention for purposes of evaluation.

Planning an Effective Intervention

What will you and others do in order to bring about the change(s) you set down in the prior step? Is there a specific order to the actions? Do the actions occur according to a specific scheme of timing? Do different persons bear responsibility for certain aspects of the intervention? The entire plan should be written out in a clear and full form. If the plan involves a sequence of steps, these should be set down before the intervention is initiated.

Part of any plan involves anticipating the final step of this process, the evaluation of effectiveness. Typically, the evaluation demands some form of data regarding the intervention and the progress of the child or children. Behavior modification plans typically require continuous data collection, a counting of the number of times the target behavior is exhibited. Data collection in the other models may involve qualitative techniques such as journalizing or writing field notes detailing daily observations of emotions and behavior. Given the time constraints facing many teachers, this process is often quite informal, relying simply on evaluative conversations between professionals about the outcomes of a given intervention.

Implementing the Intervention

Finally, the plan is put into practice. One important issue in the implementation of one or more interventions regards the question of changing the intervention along the way. Can you change course midstream? Often teachers will be midway through the behavior management plan when they realize they were off the mark in the original definition of the problem. Or maybe a different model of intervention suddenly looks more promising than the one initially chosen. Or the child's ecological systems suddenly shift in unexpected and important ways.

Can you change midstream? There is no absolute answer to this question. Traditional behavior modification may call for a full trial of the intervention including accurate data collection so that the affects may be scientifically evaluated. Despite this tradition, many talented professionals have developed the skills to alter and adapt their interventions on the fly. Doing so is no easy task, requiring sensitive and skilled judgment. This sort of adeptness and flexibility is probably less common among new practitioners of behavior management techniques.

Evaluating the Results

What are the results of the intervention? The short story involves a simple judgement about improvement or deterioration. Did things get better or worse? To what extent was the objective met? Additionally, we must be aware that interventions do not merely influence individuals and groups in ways that we anticipated. Unexpected and novel changes in behavior, emotion, and relationship come about. In fact, an intervention might solve one problem and create a new one. Attention to these subtleties is important in conducting a full evaluation.

As stated earlier, evaluation often relies on data that are collected during the actual implementation of the intervention. These data may be quantitative, such as counts of behaviors or scores on behavior rating scales. These data may be qualitative, including journals and observational field notes. Additionally, new data may be gathered during the evaluation process. Interview the child or children whose behavior was at the center of all this. Often the child or children know best whether improvement has occurred. Interview important peers or other adults who are in positions to know. Data may be gathered from many persons.

Central to the evaluation is some determination of how and why the intervention produced the results. If you can understand how the intervention influenced the child or children, then new interventions (if necessary) will be easier to design. You will hold important knowledge about what is effective or ineffective with this child or group.

We should view this final step of the long-term intervention process either as terminal or as naturally leading into the first step for another round of analysis and intervention. If the behavior problems have been solved to the satisfaction of child, teacher, parents, and others, then the process is completed. If the negative behavior or social conflict persists, or if new problems arise, then the information gathered in this final step can lead very naturally back to step one and a new definition of the problem at hand.

Examining a Case

We have just outlined a general process for both immediate and long-term intervention, attempting to provide some guidelines and direction while acknowledging the need for flexibility and innovation within the specific problem situation. This book is founded on the premise that teachers and other professionals working with children can improve behavior management skills by practicing on narrative cases of problem situations. By reading, analyzing, and discussing cases, the reader can begin to think seriously and carefully about the many possible intervention options. The cases in this book are not presented as puzzles that can be solved once and for all. They are open and exploratory, allowing for a breadth of thoughtful analysis instead of the simplicity of cookbook schemes.

In the following section, we present an initial case and provide an example of how one might develop both an immediate intervention and a long-term intervention. We present long-term interventions that draw from each of the models of behavior management (behavioral, psychodynamic, environmental, constructivist) covered in the first chapter. The case example, "I Don't Like Mondays," demonstrates the basic structure and style of the cases offered in the remainder of the book. First, an incident of problem behavior is briefly described. Then, a longer section delves into pertinent background information about the child(ren), the teacher(s) or adult(s), and the setting in which the incident took place. We provide this background information in order to emphasize the way knowledge of the relationships and events preceding the actual incident are crucial to case analysis and intervention design. The incident itself is always only a point of entry into deeper social issues and problems.

Case Example—"I Don't Like Mondays"

Incident

As Willie entered the room, he rushed to his desk, sat himself down with a loud commotion, and remarked, "I don't like Mondays. Just another day of crap for my brain." On his desk lay five math worksheets that he was to work on during homeroom period because he had failed to turn them in the week before. Willie knew that he would never complete these five worksheets in the time (10 minutes) allotted and besides, he hated math.

Mrs. Simmons, trying to ignore his initial comments, thought to herself, "Jeez, not another bad Monday with Willie." Mrs. Simmons knew that weekends were always rough on Willie.

As the other children entered the room, Tommy approached Willie, threw a baseball cap at him, and remarked, "Found this in the hallway. Next time I'll flush it down the toilet." As Susan squeezed by Willie's desk, she accidentally brushed up against him.

Willie remarked, "Get your fat ass out of my face."

Tommy replied, "You love it."

"Only with your mama," quipped Willie.

"In your dreams, hat boy," cracked Tommy. He reached out his hand and tapped the visor of Willie's baseball cap. Willie grabbed Tommy's arm. Tommy tried to pull away.

"Gentlemen!" Mrs. Simmons called from the front of the room. Willie released Tommy's arm and flashed a too-compliant smile at his teacher. Tommy grumbled and fixed his ruffled shirtsleeve. Three seconds later, once Mrs. Simmons's vigilant eyes had dropped back to the paperwork on her desk, Willie dived across his desk and grabbed Tommy by the throat. He pushed Tommy up against the wall and started pounding him in the stomach. By the time Mrs. Simmons had reached them, the two boys were engaged in a full fistfight.

Background Information

This scene occurred during the 10-minute homeroom period at the start of a Monday morning in Chester Burnett Senior High School, a large public school in an urban area. Burnett High is located in a racially mixed, economically poor neighborhood filled with symbols of both hope and misery. Boarded up windows and tenement buildings line the street where the school is located. Almost surprisingly, on the corner are two new businesses, a grocery store owned by a Pakistani family and a small coffee shop that serves up two eggs, coffee, and toast for $1.59. Unfortunately, around the corner is the most financially successful business in the neighborhood, a crack house where buyers and users come and go at all hours.

The student body of Burnett High reflects the local neighborhood: 55% African-American, 28% Latin-American, and the rest Anglo or new immigrants from Eastern Europe or India. Burnett High School has a graduation rate of 60%. This is an increase over previous years. A new school principal has provided the needed spark, rallying old and new faculty members to overhaul an outdated curriculum and try some innovative programs. For example, Burnett High School now has an entire Department of Service Learning staffed by three new teachers. These teachers work closely with a wide variety of local groups and agencies in order to bring students into nearby neighborhoods for purposes of improving the community. Students are given high school credit for work tasks ranging from serving sandwiches in a soup kitchen to learning computer skills at a local bank.

Mrs. Julia Simmons has taught home economics and English in this inner-city school district for over 25 years. As an experienced teacher of streetwise kids, Julia Simmons will tell you that she has seen many boys like Willie over the years. Some have gone on to do well. Too many have not. She speaks frequently and wearily of retirement, that final rest for the teacher who has undoubtedly earned a break. Yet in the same breath, this veteran teacher remarks about how she really wants to make a difference in the lives of her students. That's when her eyes twinkle and jump with the same enthusiasm that brought her to this job many years ago. Julia often reminisces about how the school was a better place in the old days—no guns, no drugs, especially no drugs.

Now cramped into a small room behind the library, Julia does her best to keep the students under control, with old desks crammed side by side. Julia's teaching style is a paradoxical mix of frustrated punitiveness and gentle, genuine caring. She has a saying in her room: "I walk quietly and carry a big stick." Unfortunately for her students, it means that the punishment for their inappropriate acts often far exceeds the significance of the act itself. On the other hand, Julia has been known to go out of her way to help her students, even bringing in clothing and food from home to give to those in financial need. Additionally, when not overstressed, Julia is a generous and supportive listener.

Although Tommy is one of the top students in the sophomore class, Mrs. Simmons suspects that his shiny wrapper is cleaner than its contents. Occasionally, she has seen him in the hallway, whispering and gossiping among some of the tougher boys. He hangs around with boys who are frequently arrested for small-scale drug dealing. Tommy has no police record. He never seems to get in any trouble, on the streets or in school, but he doesn't appear completely innocent. Mrs. Simmons has wondered whether Tommy instigates and promotes some of the conflicts she sees. She knows he is highly intelligent. She wonders whether he is smart enough to be conniving and slippery. In her more creative moments, Mrs. Simmons imagines that Tommy is the gangster boss behind the scenes, arranging everything in such a way that he gets away scot-free. Having no direct evidence of any wrongdoing, Mrs. Simmons keeps a tense but polite distance from Tommy. She and Tommy have never really exchanged anything more than a "Good morning."

This is not the first time Willie has started a fight. He was suspended from school on several other occasions. Willie is a tough kid with tattoos and scars covering his body; he believes they prove his manhood. Only 15, he's already lived a lifetime of torment and suffering.

Willie lives in the section of town known as "Bangtown." This area of town got its name from a bad reputation of gang fights, drugs, and violence that have occurred since the rise of crack sales in the 1980s. Willie was born to Lucia Greer when she was just 17 years old. Lucia did not know much about caring for herself, let alone a new baby. Consequently, Willie has grown up relying on himself to get things done. He learned early how to make his own breakfast, how to get around town, and most of all, how to defend himself. Lucia had dated many men after Willie was born, but none stayed longer than a few months. The latest boyfriend, Victor, has been with Lucia for about a year. For Lucia it is a stable relationship, but for Willie it is a series of beatings that usually culminate on weekends as Victor celebrates the end of the workweek by partying from Friday evening to Sunday. During this time, Willie does his best to avoid Victor by hiding in his bedroom, but nevertheless, Victor typically visits Willie to reaffirm his dominance in the house. Fortunately for Willie, Victor works the nightshift during the week, and their schedules prevent much contact.

This past weekend was no different. When Willie played the TV or his music too loud, it was Victor who came to tell him to turn it down. If Willie weren't so stubborn, he might avoid many of the arguments. But Victor, who is usually drunk, yells at Willie for only a short time before he uses his hands to resolve the disagreement.

Lucia, who works 50 to 60 hours a week, doesn't really know what is going on. When she comes home on most nights, Willie is usually sleeping and Victor is usually passed out on the sofa.

Lucia knows that Willie is a difficult child. Throughout the years, she has known that school is tough for Willie. He had difficulties in learning to read. He can't get along with the other students. He flies off the handle at the slightest provocation. By the fourth grade, he had already lost interest in school. Lucia could relate to this because she too had difficulty in school and eventually dropped out when she was 15 years old. As she watches her son grow up, Lucia sees him go through periods of deep depression. His chronic unhappiness is difficult for her to bear. Sometimes she feels an overwhelming sense of guilt, as if it must be all her fault.

Julia Simmons knows Willie and Lucia well. She has spent evenings on the telephone with Lucia discussing Willie—his behavior, his academics, and his future. Julia often discusses Willie's problems in depth with him before school. But Willie is cautious never to mention the beatings that he receives at home. He feels great shame that Victor beats him.

Immediate Intervention

If possible, Willie and Tommy must be separated. Safety is a major consideration. Certainly, the teacher can firmly tell the boys to break it up. Yet she must also make a quick decision about whether her safety or the safety of any students will be compromised by her physical intervention. Should she try to separate the combatants? She must decide quickly. If she is unable to stop the fight, she will need to clear the other classmates out of the room and call for help if possible. Given Mrs. Simmons's age and the size of these two adolescent boys, we can envision her directing the boys very firmly to stop while simultaneously moving other students out of the room. She sends a reliable student to the office to retrieve the personnel necessary (the assistant principal, school police officer, etc.) to pull the boys apart.

Once the fight is over, the combatants will need to be removed from the class and separated from each other. Removing Willie and Tommy from the situation would allow them to cool down and the class to return to peace and order so that learning can resume. Julia Simmons has a strong relationship with Willie. Once he calms down, it would be ideal if she could be the one to talk him through the entire sequence of events, discussing both his feelings and his behavior. Since this teacher does not have much trust built up with Tommy, it may be best for someone who knows him better to talk to him.

Long-Term Intervention

The conflict described in this case requires not only immediate action but also a careful plan of long-term intervention to prevent similar incidents from occurring in the future. Given Willie's history of fighting in school and Mrs. Simmons's suspicion that Tommy may be a prominent instigator of conflicts, such a plan makes sense. In this section, we generate long-term intervention options using each of the four models. We utilize all four models in order to display their use. Typically, a long-term intervention will involve only one, two, or perhaps three models.

Psychodynamic Model

According to the psychodynamic model, Willie's violent behavior demonstrates and acts out some very powerful underlying feelings. An incident such as this is viewed as a crucial opportunity for learning, a chance for a caring and skilled adult to guide a young person through powerful emotions to self-knowledge. Anger seems to be the most obvious emotion, but we can also anticipate that Willie may feel sadness, jealousy, a personal sense of inadequacy, or rejection. Assessment and intervention will involve talking with Willie to help him express, understand, and find more constructive ways of handling those feelings. This process involves the development of an intimate form of trust between student and teacher. In this regard, we can see that the psychodynamic model of intervention does not rely on one-shot cures but involves the gradual development of a therapeutic relationship over time. It is possible that we should refer Willie to a qualified psychotherapist for ongoing therapy.

Through the conversation, Mrs. Simmons wants to guide and support Willie to develop a greater understanding of his own emotions, the source of those emotions, and the way he expressed those emotions through physical violence. We ultimately want to help him to look closely at ways of handling his feelings that do not involve violence. Additionally, Mrs. Simmons brings with her an awareness that Willie tends to seem emotionally unsteady on Mondays. She suspects that something negative is happening at home on the weekends. If a moment arises in her conversation where Willie seems to be trusting her and looking to her for guidance, she will tell him her observations and ask him if anything is going on at home. She must be aware that this is a very delicate question that is very likely raise his defenses.

Two specific issues concerning Tommy must be addressed. First, Tommy's feelings and actions must be taken into consideration. From the teasing through the fight itself, he was a full participant in this incident. A trusted and qualified professional (perhaps a guidance counselor or teacher) should talk to Tommy privately about this incident and his feelings toward and relationship with Willie. He needs to become aware of the connection between his own feelings toward Willie and the way he treated Willie. Additionally, given the way Tommy hangs around with a criminal crowd in the hallways, it is very possible that he has already become involved in delinquent activity. His affiliation with a negative crowd should be questioned and even challenged. We can envision a trusted adult asking Tommy serious questions, for example, "What do you want for your future?" or "Why do you hang around with the kids who deal drugs?" These are very personal and confrontational questions. If they are to be asked, they must be asked by an adult whom Tommy views as caring, as acting in his best interests. If these questions are merely thrown at Tommy in an accusatory fashion by someone whom Tommy does not trust, he is not likely to view the intervention as helpful. He is likely to defend, hide his activities, and continue down a bad path.

Environmental Model

There are clear indications that some academic tasks are experienced as boring or frustrating by Willie. He does describe the school day as "another load of crap for my brain." He has failed to complete his math work from the week before. This makes us wonder what personal interests he has and how these can be connected to the curriculum to make the work more personally meaningful. We need to talk to him about this. We may need to talk to his math teacher to find out more about Willie's performance in that class. Is he frustrated? Is he keeping up with the work? Does he need tutoring or other support?

In regard to the physical layout of the classroom during homeroom period, maybe Willie and Tommy should not sit near one another, at least until the heated emotions settle. Additionally, we wonder if the physical distance between Mrs. Simmons and her students is too great. She may have greater influence if her desk is not so far removed from the students' desks.

Socially, it is obvious that the relationship between the two boys involved is tense and conflict ridden. It might be best to sit these two boys down with Mrs. Simmons and discuss their differences and gripes. Additionally, given the cliquish nature of teenage peer groups, we should investigate whether the friction between Willie and Tommy is indicative of larger conflicts between groups of friends. It is very possible that a clash between two groups of peers or within a single group is playing out in the form of a one-on-one fight. This can be investigated by talking to the two boys, talking to other students, and asking the advice of other teachers who keep close track of the networks of friendships among the various students.

Constructivist Model

In this model, Mrs. Simmons would view the fight as a sign that the unity, respect, and caring among students in the class (and perhaps in the school more broadly) needs to be studied, discussed, and improved. The classroom network of relationships, the intimate community of students, is failing in a significant way. A fight is viewed as a conflict between the two boys involved and as a classroom community issue that impacts and involves all.

Mrs. Simmons might first reflect on her own role, examining the way she is talking to and treating her students. Is she living up to her value of reciprocal respect? Despite her best intentions, she must look at the ways that she is not supporting or encouraging respectful and equal relationships between students. Her questioning, in particular, should focus on her relationships with and her affect on the two boys involved in the fight.

Since the violence has threatened and disrupted the classroom community, Mrs. Simmons may wish for Willie (and perhaps Tommy) to receive some sort of consequences that are closely related to the offense. Most likely, she will open this issue up for discussion among all the students in the class. The act of opening up the issue for discussion encourages ownership and responsibility among all the students.

The discussion of the incident among the entire class should be orderly but open. One person speaks at a time. All voices are honored and encouraged. All must speak in respectful ways. The discussion has a bit of a New England town meeting feel to it. The teacher facilitates, guiding the conversation gently toward a conclusion that brings about unity and allows the group to continue to work in safety and comfort.

What would be said in such a group meeting is not known. The goal is to help the students inquire seriously about the ongoing conflicts and general weaknesses in their web of relationships. The discussion may be emotional. Mrs. Simmons may wish to bring in a guidance counselor or other supportive professional who is trusted by these students. The discussion must be practical and constructive, leading ultimately to a group decision on specific actions for improvement. During this process, Mrs. Simmons must remain open to the fact that the students may comment on or critique specific things she has done. They may claim she is unfair or too controlling. They may criticize other aspects of their school. If the teacher can open herself up to this process as a chance to learn about herself and to learn how to better meet the needs of her students, then she can benefit from the students' words of criticism.

Behavioral Model

The most likely use of the behavioral model would be a functional analysis of the classroom variables that promote the negative behavior, both Willie's assault on Tommy and Tommy's teasing. Such an analysis would only be possible if the negative behaviors in question (i.e., the assault and the teasing) are fairly common for these two boys. While we have some suspicion that the conflict between Tommy and Willie may be ongoing, we have no evidence in this case that these two specific behaviors are being exhibited frequently by these boys. For this reason, a functional analysis does not seem like a likely choice. The use of a behavioral contract through which one or both of these boys earns privileges or rewards may be considered appropriate.

SUMMARY OF CASE ANALYSIS

Based primarily on the psychodynamic, environmental, and constructivist models, we can quickly summarize our case analysis within the five steps detailed earlier.

1. *Assessing the problem.* The surface problem seems to be a heated personal conflict between Tommy and Willie. This relational difficulty is probably the tip of a number of larger icebergs. It is likely that both Tommy and Willie are going through some personal struggles of their own. Willie's family situation involving the abuse by his mother's boyfriend is painful for him. Tommy's apparent criminal activity is a growing problem for him. Additionally, as a broader ecological issue, we are aware that some between-group or within-group struggles may be occurring among networks of peers. All these hypotheses require additional investigation, but we are pretty sure that discussions with Tommy and Willie will bring many of the details of these three background "icebergs" to light.

2. *Formulating objectives of intervention.* For the surface issue concerning the conflict between Tommy and Willie, our goal is to help each of these boys learn to handle interpersonal difficulties without fighting. In regard to the three beneath the surface "icebergs" (i.e., Willie's family problems, Tommy's apparent criminal activities, and apparent group conflicts among the larger student body), our goal is to find out if these suspected problems are really serious and, therefore, require some sort of intervention.

3. *Planning an effective intervention.* Four separate intervention plans should be implemented:

   a. Willie—Individual Life Space Intervention or a brief counseling session with a trusted, qualified professional (Mrs. Simmons)
   b. Tommy—Individual Life Space Intervention or a brief counseling session with a trusted, qualified professional (a guidance counselor or teacher)

c. Tommy and Willie—Possibly a combined counseling session to discuss conflicts and work out differences

d. Mrs. Simmons's homeroom—A discussion with the entire class, led by Mrs. Simmons and a guidance counselor, about how to improve the unity and cooperation among the group

4. *Implementing the intervention*

5. *Evaluating the results.* About 2 to 3 weeks after the above interventions have been completed, Mrs. Simmons should meet with both boys individually and together to evaluate the effectiveness of the interventions. What has happened? Have the two boys fought with each other or anyone? How are the two boys getting along with each other? What is the status of the "iceberg" issues? Mrs. Simmons (and perhaps other school personnel) should monitor both the surface issue (the Tommy-Willie relationship) and the iceberg issues on a regular basis. Observing student behavior in class and in the hallways and holding discussions with various students about these issue will allow these professionals to keep a finger to the pulse of these problems.

References

Danforth, S. (1997). Autobiography as critical pedagogy: Locating myself in class-based oppression. *Teaching Education, 9*(1), 3–14.

Harrington, H. L., Quinn-Leering, K., & Hodson, L. (1996). Written case analyses and critical reflection. *Teaching and Teacher Education, 12*(1), 25–37.

Wood, M. M., & Long, N. J. (1991). *Life space intervention*. Austin, TX: Pro-Ed.

PART II

BEHAVIOR MANAGEMENT CASES

CASE 1

THE AFTER-SCHOOL SCHOOL

THE INCIDENT

"The simple truth is that Pauline's mother doesn't care!" exclaimed Trish Curran, the director of the August Tutorial Program (ATP). The frustrated woman looked across her desk at her coworker, Abbey Gajar: "Pauline's behavior was terrible all last week. She refused to do any of her work. I sent her to time-out. She called me a bitch and ran around the parking lot like a little savage. I sent notes home on Tuesday and Wednesday. Got no reply from Mom."

"Did you——" Abbey paused to lean back in her seat and cast a quick look through the large glass window to see how the children were doing. On the other side of the glass was the ATP classroom, where 20 fourth and fifth graders sat at six broad tables. A single adult, an elderly volunteer known affectionately as Grandma, was monitoring the students as they worked (or pretended to work) on homework assignments. Convinced that the group of children seemed relatively quiet, Abbey continued, "Um, did you call her?"

"Yes, I called her. Left a message on the machine and she never called back. I get so tired of moms that don't care about their——"

Boom! A loud crash sounded across the classroom. Then came a high-pitched blare of laughter. Abbey hopped up and ran from the office into the classroom. Trish followed at her heels. The laughing children were gathered in a close circle around one of the tables. Abbey and Trish pushed their way through to the center, where they found Pauline sprawled on the ground, her skirt looped up over her head and her feet kicking high in the air. One of the large tables had collapsed down to the floor. Grandma was on her knees struggling to pull Pauline's skirt down to conceal the young girl's underwear. Pauline angrily squirmed to get away from Grandma.

BACKGROUND INFORMATION

What happened? Pauline was again refusing to do her work. Grandma didn't see Pauline place the small headphones on her ears and turn on the portable CD player. A group of older boys seated at her table repeatedly challenged her to dance on the table top. Knowing this would only get her in trouble, Pauline declined repeatedly. The boys continued encouraging her to dance. Finally, in an effort to impress these boys, Pauline climbed up on the table. She didn't even dance. She stood momentarily still and her face flushed red with the embarrassment. It was obvious to all that she wished that she had never let the boys coax her into it. Suddenly, with a groan and a crackle, the rickety old table surrendered beneath Pauline's feet, sending both girl and table to the floor in a dramatic crash.

A casual observer would have noticed that 15 seconds before Pauline climbed on top of the frail table, less than half of the ATP students were actually working on their homework. Many slept with their heads on their folded arms. Others leaned their heads together and traded whispers and giggles. Pauline was far from the only child who was not productively engaged in academic work.

The ATP staff has struggled to get the students to do their homework. The children are often restless and disgruntled. Many feel that they have already spent the day at school, and they do not want to go to the "after-school school."

Most of the students were referred to the program by their home school for failing to turn in homework on a regular basis. With parental approval, a student is enrolled in the program. At the end of the regular school day, buses carry the students from their home schools to the ATP classroom located at the back of the old vocational high school. The ATP offers a 1-hour study time supervised by two staff members and an occasional volunteer for the third, fourth, and fifth grade children who attend.

The ATP staff members are not certified teachers. They are paid the hourly wage of teacher aides. Abbey and Trish fulfill the typical profile of ATP staff members: young, middle-class women who do not live in Metcalf Heights and are pursing degrees in education at a local university.

The August Tutorial Program opened only 2 months before this incident. It is one of six after-school tutoring programs set up by the Metcalf Heights School District, a small urban district located on the near northern edge of a midsized city. Metcalf Heights, once considered a suburb of the city, is now virtually indistinguishable from the north side of the city itself. The population is 60% African-American, 20% new immigrants from Russia and other Eastern European countries, and 20% Anglo-American. The median family income is barely above the federal poverty level.

Ten years ago, Metcalf Heights was a busy industrial area. Three chemical plants and a small glass factory employed over half of the town residents. The town's unemployment rate was under 4%. Now the unemployment rate is over 20%. Only the glass plant remains since the chemical industry moved to Mexico. Many families soon moved out of Metcalf Heights, too, leaving the town for job opportunities elsewhere. The population of Metcalf Heights has decreased 32% in the past decade. Primarily the most economically disadvantaged residents remain.

The Metcalf Heights School District is in the midst of a comprehensive reform effort spurred chiefly by a series of critical articles printed in the local newspaper, the *Daily Herald*. The *Herald* annually publishes a "school report card" in which they evaluate local school districts on the basis of a number of factors including standardized achievement scores. In previous years, Metcalf Heights had been highlighted as one of the most promising urban districts in the region. Their programs had been described as progressive and innovative. Due to a sudden 2-year slide in standardized scores, the *Herald* gave the district a D+ and launched an investigation to determine why the Metcalf Heights schools were seemingly moving backward. This investigation produced a series of scathing newspaper reports describing the central administration of the district as "a poorly tuned, well-fattened, and bureaucratically dense machine that has lost touch with its students and lost control of its teachers."

The district responded with a program of reform that includes no changes in the central administrative ranks but effectively increases the amount of time many students receive instruction. Almost half of the schools were switched to a lengthened school year, adding 20 full days to the calendar. Based on the assumption that students need to complete more homework to score higher on standardized exams, six after-school tutorial programs were instituted immediately. Plans call for 10 more within the next 2 years.

Pauline is an African-American. She is a fourth grader at Airport Elementary School. Her teachers consider her an extremely bright young girl who inconsistently applies her attention and abilities to academic tasks. She is often described by teachers as disrespectful to adults and emotionally labile. Her peers describe her as funny and lively, but too gossipy. She often jumps from social group to social group, spreading rumors and pushing emotional buttons. According to the standardized achievement tests, Pauline is working a year above grade level in reading and 2 years in mathematics. She was referred to the ATP because she rarely turns in her homework assignments. Additionally, the Airport School staff felt that some extra attention and encouragement might turn Pauline on to academic learning and her own abilities.

At the ATP, the staff has struggled to deal with the tremendous number of students who do not really work on their homework during the tutorial period. Abbey and Trish have come to accept the behavior of students who refuse to work in relatively calm and passive ways. For example, they usually do not attempt to roust students who nap on folded arms. Low-volume talking, while against the official rules of the program, has been allowed by the staff. In response to Pauline's loud and disruptive behavior, Abbey and Trish have tried to redirect her back to her work. Sometimes Pauline has taken this as a message to avoid her work in a much quieter way. She has spent many afternoons silently drawing pictures on her notebook.

When Pauline has not quieted down, the ATP staff members have followed the standard procedures for dealing with a disruptive student. She has been directed to sit in the time-out chair adjacent to the office at the edge of the classroom. Usually, Pauline has gone to time-out throwing out a few mumbled insults on the way. Students are only allowed to return from time-out if they agree that they will return to their seat and work. Pauline has spent many long afternoons sitting in the time-out chair. One recent afternoon she completely refused to go to time-out. She raced out the door and spent the next 30 minutes zigzagging in and out of parked cars like a slalom skier while an exasperated Trish tried unsuccessfully to catch her.

CASE 2

BLINDED BY SCIENCE

THE INCIDENT

As Charlie Jameson sat in science class that May morning, the last thing that he heard before passing out was a loud thump; it was the sound of Rashon Rickson's science textbook hitting him on the head.

Rashon had worked for the previous 2 weeks to develop a model of the Mars *Pathfinder,* along with a working model of the rover. The model, built to scale, included Martian-like rocks, one with the name Barnacle Bill. In a matter of minutes, Rashon's exacting work was scattered to pieces on the ground, with Charlie towering over the mess like a giant who had just destroyed a miniature village. Unable to speak, Rashon just stared in amazement, his lower lip quivered with sadness. Meanwhile, Charlie looked on and let out a bellowing laugh. As his laugh echoed within Rashon's ears, Rashon's face slowly became red with anger. Charlie then very calmly took his seat and began to finish up his own project. Seething with anger, Rashon grabbed his science textbook, walked up behind Charlie's desk, and with all of his weight slammed it on Charlie's head. As Charlie fell to the ground, Mr. Saxton, the science teacher, ran to grab him, but missed and instead landed on the pile of children who had gathered around the incident. Mr. Saxton was visibly shaken by the incident. Ordering children back to their desks while simultaneously grabbing Rashon by the arm, Mr. Saxton's entire body was quaking.

"Jay, go to the office and tell Mr. Griffin to call an ambulance and tell him to get down here. Now!" Mr. Saxton barked to the student closest to the door.

BACKGROUND INFORMATION

It wasn't the first time that Charlie and Rashon had been involved in an altercation, and it probably won't be the last. Charlie was the class bully. Everyone—the students in the class, the teachers in the school, and the principal—kept an eye out for Charlie. Charlie's sheer size made him stand out in this fifth-grade class. He would intimidate any child who stood in his way. Charlie was the boss of the students and often got his way through a threatening glance. Charlie was too familiar with the in-school-suspension (ISS) procedures and did not fear being sent home for hitting or fighting. Charlie's dad, Henry "Rock" Jameson, had instilled in his son to use whatever it took to be a "winner" in life. Charlie was often heard telling his victims, "Suckers like you make up the losers in the world."

According to most kids in the class, Rashon was a "geek." He was a good-looking fifth grader, but his glasses and his sweater vests often made him look like a professor. Rashon's interest in science led him to spend long hours searching the Internet and prevented him from socializing with other students. In fact, the exactness of his *Pathfinder* model came about because he was able to study pictures from the various Web sites that kept him apprised of the latest developments from the Mars landing. Rashon was the most intelligent child in class, often outsmarting Mr. Saxton. Rashon was also one of the most despised kids, because he flaunted his intelligence and money. For every trophy that he won, he would proudly walk around the room placing it in the faces of his losing competitors. For Rashon, winning intellectual endeavors validated his worth. Extremely competitive, his parents were often more proud of his accolades than the actual projects. His dad, Zachary Rickson, a computer systems manager at a high-tech firm, paid little attention to Rashon except when he brought home a prize. His mother, a real estate agent, often had little time to spend with Rashon because her career required that she work many evenings and weekends. A millionaire real estate agent, Tina Rickson was always after the next property, the next client, the next deal.

Why Rashon didn't fear Charlie remains a mystery. Rashon was Charlie's antithesis in life, and mixing the two often resulted in Rashon's ripped clothes and Charlie's satisfactory glow. Oddly enough, in a number of ways Charlie and Rashon were a lot alike. Both had parents who valued competitiveness and cherished winning. Both boys learned that it was primarily after some incident (Charlie's fights and Rashon's trophies) that their parents would take the time to acknowledge and talk to them.

On the morning of the above incident, Rashon and his father were eating breakfast together. Like most mornings, Mom was already at the office. The father and son did not talk. Rashon ate cereal while reading a science book, and Zachary drank his cappuccino while tapping away on a laptop computer. Each was busy living in his own little world, until Rashon had an accident. He was pouring milk on his second bowl of cereal when it spilled. The milk made a quick path to Zachary's laptop.

"What are you doing? Do you know the damage liquids can do to this computer?" Zachary shouted. Zachary had been up most of the night working on a computer program, and it may have been fatigue that caused him to yell at Rashon. Rashon grabbed for a towel and tried to soak up the milk while pleading for his father's forgiveness. Zachary continued to yell. Then something odd happened. Normally by now Rashon would be in tears from his father's scolding, but on this day Rashon fought back the tears and yelled at his father.

"All that you care about is your damn computer!" he shouted as he bolted out the door. Zachary called him back, realizing that there was some truth to his statement, but it was too late; Rashon was gone. In another part of town, a different father-son scenario was playing out in the Jameson household. At breakfast, Charlie and his father, Rock, got into an argument. Rock was angry with Charlie because he stole cigarettes from his coat pocket and smoked them in the basement. Rock actually didn't catch Charlie smoking; in fact, he had found cigarette butts behind the furnace. As he yelled at Charlie during breakfast, the boy's tears fell into his cereal. Despite the overwhelming evidence, Charlie denied the allegations. His denials only intensified Rock's anger, until finally he slapped Charlie in the face.

Rock loved his son, but he often used the same tough disciplinary methods that his father had used on him. He used punishment to solve most of his family problems. As Charlie ran out the door that morning, he told his father that he hated him and that he wished he were dead. Rock felt bad and called out to his son, but it was too late for apologies; Charlie had already pedaled his bike out of sight.

"Damn, another time that I screwed up," Rock mumbled under his breath.

CASE 3

Getting Caught

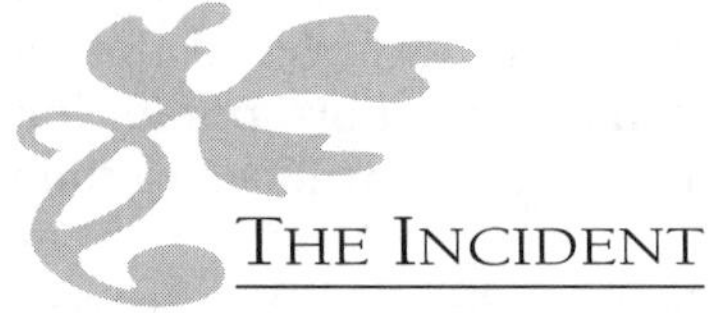

The Incident

As Mr. Conners, the teacher in the self-contained behavior disorders (BD) class at Stewart High School, is at his desk busily grading papers, his students are hard at work at their desks. David and Tommy are sitting next to each other discussing how attractive Susie is looking in her provocative, pink sweater.

"Boy, I'd like to get me some of that," Tommy remarks to David.

David agrees and says to Tommy, "Watch this!" David then moves up two seats so that he is now seated directly behind Susie. After giving Tommy a smirk, he whispers in Susie's ear, "I can't wait to squeeze your love melons." He then tells her that he plans to follow her home to get some "action." "Don't worry. No one will ever see us," he adds. Having been a victim of sexual abuse in the past, Susie becomes very frightened and immediately runs to Mr. Conners's desk to tell him about David's comments. Mr. Conners immediately turns around and glares at David, who is now back in his original seat.

David looks up and in a surprised voice says, "What?"

"In the hall," Mr. Conners calls out.

As David is walking toward the door, Tommy laughs and calls out, "You're busted." In the hall, David is confronted about the incident by Mr. Conners. Mr. Conners fires a series of questions, one after the other, but David denies each one and then begins to cry. Through his tears he is heard to say, "Everyone hates me. I never get a fair shake."

Background Information

David is a tall, good-looking young man, who has been in and out of residential treatment centers and special schools for the past 5 years. Now 16, he has been in Mr. Conners's self-contained behavior disordered classroom for 3 months. His entry into Mr. Conners's room did not come easy for David. It was only after pleas were made for him to move to a less restrictive environment by his educational advocate, Billy Russo, that David was placed in Mr. Conners's classroom. His prior placement was in the Central Behavioral Center (CBC), a center that provides a very tight structure for students with severe behavioral problems.

The CBC uses a "level system" for behavior management, with level 1 (a punishment level) being the most restrictive and level 7 being the least restrictive. Using this system, students who enter are placed in level 2 and must earn their way upward to level 7 to gain entry to a self-contained behavior disorders class in a local public school in the Woodward School District. During each period of the day, students are awarded 5 points for appropriate social behavior. If the student earns 55 or more points for the day and continues this for 10 school days, that student advances to the next highest level.

David has been attending the CBC for the past 2 years. What expedited his move was the work of Billy Russo. While at the CBC, David had earned his way up to level 4, despite falling back to lower levels at times. When Mr. Russo was assigned to David by the state of Wisconsin, David had just earned his level 4 status. As his educational advocate, Mr. Russo immediately went to the CBC to meet David, speak to his teachers, and tour the center. Mr. Russo came away from this initial meeting feeling very concerned about David. Mr. Russo felt that in David's case, the CBC's behavioral system was ineffective, possibly doing more harm than good. After several follow-up visits, Mr. Russo finally persuaded the staff at the CBC to place David in a self-contained classroom at Stewart High School for a trial period of 3 months. At this meeting, the staff from the CBC were reluctant, but under the threat of a "due process" by Mr. Russo, they agreed to the trial period. Mr. Conners, present at the meeting, was also reluctant to bend the rules for David, but under pressure from his supervisor, he agreed to the trial period.

It is important to note that at this meeting, David's CBC teacher, Jan Hallson, brought up three prior incidents in her classroom where David displayed inappropriate behavior. In the first incident, when David was wrestling with two other students, one being a young woman, David was accused of grabbing her in her "private" parts. David said it was an accident and that he meant nothing by it. In another situation, David was accused of sending one of his teachers love notes. The notes had sexual overtones to them, and Mrs. Kackasaw, the teacher, viewed it as a "schoolboy crush." David, however, was devastated when Mrs. Kackasaw finally confronted him and told him to stop sending her notes. Listless, David did not perform well in school during the month that followed. Finally, in a third incident, David was accused of using the Internet at the school to download pornography. Although no one observed David doing this, many teachers felt that he was one of the few children in the school who was knowledgeable enough to commit such an act. In addition, Mrs. Hallson overheard her students discussing how David had downloaded "dirty" pictures. She confronted David, but he denied involvement in the incident.

In addition, David's social worker, Raine Tuttle, was quick to mention David's deteriorating home life. From the records, Raine indicated that David comes from a single-parent home in which he lives with his mother. She also noted that David's father had left the household when David was 10 after a series of incidents of physical and sexual abuse. Raine claimed that David's mother had thrown the father out of the house after a drunken episode in which he broke David's arm. Raine also pointed out that David's mom is currently having a lot of difficulty with David. Apparently, David has twice run away from home and does not adhere to his mother's curfew of 11 o'clock. When his mother confronts him about his behavior David often states that now he is the "man of the house."

Three months have since passed since the placement decision. The scenario documented in this case is David's first major behavioral incident. David has displayed minor behavior problems since being placed in Mr. Conners's room. For instance, almost daily David complains that his class work is too difficult for him, despite the fact that David performed quite well on a number of standardized achievement tests. David has also been involved in two loud arguments, both involving another student calling him names. Once David was caught carving his name into a desk with a knife. Although Mr. Conners claims that David is not much of a problem, compared to the other eight students in the class, he still feels that David has much improvement to make before he can be mainstreamed in regular education classes. Mr. Conners notes that David displays a pattern whereby he has a number of days of excellent behavior interrupted by a day or two of unruly and disruptive behavior.

CASE 4

PEOPLE CHANGE

THE INCIDENT

As Vito rolled down the hall in his wheelchair, he felt the eyes of his classmates watching him. Some students stopped talking and stared at him like motorists moving past an automobile accident. A few students called, "Hey, Vito." When Vito reached his destination, biology class, Mr. Cronwell greeted him with a cheery "Hello," but Vito did not reply. Instead, he moved to his special desk, the one without the chair, and watched his fellow students file into the room. As the second bell rang, the last few students hurriedly found their desks. Taking her seat next to Vito, Susan whispered, "Hello," to Vito.

Immediately, Vito exploded with a series of angry statements: "Don't talk to me. You're just like the rest of 'em. I don't need your pity." With all eyes now fixed on him, Vito looked around and said, "Screw all of you." With that comment, he quickly moved his wheelchair into the aisle and headed for the door.

Mr. Cronwell quickly positioned himself between Vito and the door. Intercepting Vito, Mr. Cronwell empathetically said, "Look Vito, the kids are just trying to be nice."

Vito, who was now becoming increasingly angrier, shouted out, "I don't want your niceness or pity or help." As Mr. Cronwell escorted Vito through the door and into the hallway, he again pleaded with Vito to calm down and keep his voice down, but Vito refused and shouted, "Kiss my ass!" as he wheeled down the hall. Mr. Cronwell just watched and shook his head, thinking to himself how much Vito had changed over the past 8 months.

BACKGROUND INFORMATION

A high school sports hero, Vito is now only a semblance of his former self. He was the captain of the football team and one of the school's fastest athletes in track. He was also a scholar-athlete who excelled in his English and science classes and was always on the honor roll. Now he has trouble learning new information that is abstract in nature. He was a popular student who would light up the room upon entering it. Now he sours the happy moods and either speaks with spite to others or refuses to talk at all. This drastic change in Vito came about because of "the accident."

One late November night, Vito's parents, Debbie and Frank, received the phone call that all parents dread. It was from a police officer who was calling to tell them that Vito had been in a terrible accident. As his parents hurriedly dressed and rushed to the hospital, Debbie's first thought was about Vito's heavy drinking. Vito began drinking and experimenting with illegal drugs when he was 15. Now, 2 years later, his drinking binges were occurring on a more frequent basis. Vito's athleticism and personality made him a popular person to invite to parties. Unfortunately, Vito's mix of drugs and alcohol made for a dangerous combination. On that particular night, Vito went out with friends to celebrate the team's latest victory. As he gave his mom a hug before leaving, Debbie had an uneasy feeling. Debbie and Frank felt that drinking and getting drunk was just part of growing up. Both Debbie and Frank drank on weekends when they were in high school, and although it was a bit unnerving, they saw no harm in Vito's celebrations. How things have changed. Debbie now coordinates the local chapter of Mothers Against Drunk Drivers and Frank works with the local after-school program, which provides midnight basketball for youth.

The car, driven by a drunken friend, smashed into a tree, and Vito went headfirst through the windshield. He was the most seriously injured of the group. Miraculously, his friends Ned, Matt, and Pete suffered only minor injuries. At first it was touch and go; Vito spent 2 weeks in a coma while hooked up to a life-support system. It took 3 months in rehabilitation before Vito was well enough to be sent home.

After 3 months in intense rehabilitation, Vito emerged a different person. By that time many of his friendships had waned and his attitude had soured. There were many sleepless nights for Vito when he would ask himself, "Why should I live?" Despite his large group of friends, Vito was often ashamed when they would visit him, and there were quite a few days when Vito refused to see any visitors.

Before long, Vito's mother was talking to him about going back to school. After a series of evaluations, it was determined that Vito required speech therapy, because of his facial reconstructive surgery, and some consultation services from the special education teacher, Martha Pearson, because of his head injury. According to Martha, "Whatever Vito did poorly prior to the accident, he would now probably perform worse." She understood how head injuries often amplify the weaker cognitive ability areas, making them worse. In Vito's case, his occasional bouts of depression before the accident now became more frequent and more pronounced. In addition to these problems, he also suffered a spinal cord injury resulting in the loss of use of his legs and restricting him to a wheelchair.

When Vito started back to school a month ago, some 7 months after the accident, he received a lot of support from teachers and students. In fact, he was actually embarrassed by all of the attention that he received. Because he tired easily, he started back to school on a part-time basis. On most days, he was permitted to go to the nurse's office to take short naps. While his friends tried not to treat him differently, things had undoubtedly changed. Vito could not attend physical education or play sports. He used the school's elevator to get to his classes. Vito's fatigue also prevented him from participating in many of the after-school programs. Worst of all, Vito could not go out with his friends like he used to. He and his friends were now restricted to his house or neighborhood. Through all these changes, Vito tried to remain optimistic, but over time, his new limitations began to take their toll on him. He became sullen and bitter about his life and his relationships. He felt that he had lost everything he loved about his life. And he felt overwhelmed by hopelessness and anger.

CASE 5

God Bless the Children

The Incident

Julie's children had had fights over toys before, but those were nothing compared to the fight that occurred in church this past Sunday. Describing the incident to the twins' day care teacher, Brian Owens, Julie's voice began to crack as tears filled her eyes. "What am I going to do?" asked Julie through her tears. "Tell me everything that happened," replied Brian in a soft, calming voice.

It all began when Father John began his sermon. "And the Lord said, 'All the people of the world shall be welcome into his kingdom,'" shouted Father in a loud, commanding voice. Suddenly a child's shrieking voice came from the back pews. As Father paused to catch his breath, he heard the little voice cry out, "Don't touch my t-ex dinosus. It's my t-ex." An embarrassed Julie Wilcom looked down, gave an her boys an angry look, and followed that up with a long "Shhhhhh." Her twins, Byron and Shelby, unfazed by the threat, continued their tug-of-war over the twisted plastic dinosaur. When she grabbed the toy from their hands, her anger temporarily quieted the boys, but soon both were tugging on her arm asking her for it back in loud, hushed voices. By now, it became apparent that Byron and Shelby were not only interfering with her ability to listen to the sermon but also disturbing other parishioners sitting next to her. As Father John went on with his sermon, she grabbed their two little hands and hurriedly raced down the aisle to the back of the church. Julie was walking so quickly that the boys' little feet were just barely able to keep up. Once through the church doors and into the vestibule, Julie's seething anger overcame her, and she angrily lectured the boys about yelling in church. "What are you boys fighting about?" she demanded.

"But he took it first," stammered Byron.

"No, it's my toy," replied Shelby.

"Stop it, both of you," Julie said as she interrupted their argument. "You boys embarrassed me in front of Father John and the rest of the members of the church. Why don't you ever behave in church?" Then she realized that often there is no forthcoming rationale for the behavior of 5-year-olds. As tears ran down their small faces, Julie told them that she loved them and then walked back up the aisle to their seats. As Julie sat down, Father John, who was just finishing his sermon, remarked, "And let us not forget that the children are our future. So God bless and protect them." With that, Julie let out a chuckle as she looked down at her children who were once again pulling and tugging at the toy dinosaur.

BACKGROUND INFORMATION

Julie had tried a number of times before to bring her children to church without incident, but every time they came, the boys managed to put on a repeat performance that included hitting, yelling, and crying. Fellow parishioners had suggested that Julie use the "crying room" (a soundproof room in which you could hear the service, but no one else could hear you), but she patiently explained that she wanted the boys to become familiar with mass because next year they would enter the church kindergarten and would have to participate in the mass. Other parents had also brought their children to Sunday masses, and Julie felt that her children had a right to be in church during mass, too. In fact, Julie would often pack books and toys just in case the boys became bored.

Byron and Shelby are all set to enter the St. Matthew's Elementary School next year. They currently attend Reedville's Montessori School for Children (a day care) and have excelled, cognitively and socially, at using the multimodal approaches to learning. Although Julie believes that their behavior has become worse since attending school, she is often hesitant to mention it to their day care teacher. Their teacher, Brian, has told Julie, "Young children should not be pushed into something that they are not developmentally ready for." Brian then went on to explain, "Children need time to be children. They need to grow, develop, and mature before they are capable of fully using or following adult rules."

The phrase *children need time to be children* really sticks with Julie. Her father, a general in the army, required that she grow up following a strict code of conduct, resulting in her growing up "too quickly." She often looks back with regret at having missed so much of her childhood because she was busy doing chores, like cleaning the house or doing the laundry. She did not have very many friends while growing up and blames her father for her lost childhood. Perhaps it was because of these experiences that she wanted just the opposite for her children and, in fact, that she chose Reedville's Montessori school for them.

At home, Byron and Shelby have always been together, particularly since Macon, Julie's ex-husband, moved out. At first the boys were deeply affected by their parents' breakup, but over time they seemed to adjust. Initially, one or both boys would cry at night because Macon was not there to tuck them in; however, within months both boys seemed better adjusted.

Although now better at dealing with the divorce, the boys still talk about getting Mom and Dad back together and often become depressed when they return from weekend visits with their father. Despite their turmoil over the divorce, the boys have become emotionally closer to one another.

"You know, Brian," Julie says, finishing her story, "over the past few days, the boys' behavior has gotten worse. They had a fight on Tuesday, two on Wednesday, one on Friday, and three fights yesterday." Brian is well aware of their fighting, but feels that this is a behavior that the boys will outgrow. As he listens to the story, he notices the two boys in the corner fighting over the same truck. "Look at them. Just what am I going to do?" an exasperated Julie asks. At this point, Brian, who is at a loss for words, simply shrugs his shoulders.

C A S E **6**

When Is Collaboration Not Collaboration?

The Incident

"Boring, boring," was Stanley's reply to Mr. Gaskins's question.

"Let me ask you again," Mr. Gaskins repeated. "In this experiment, what happened when we put water in a bottle and placed it in the freezer?"

"The damn thing blew up," Stanley shot back.

"No, that's not the answer I am looking for and don't use that language in this class," Mr. Gaskins replied. With his comment, Stanley laid his head back down on his desk and closed his eyes. Out of aggravation, Mr. Gaskins walked up to Stanley's desk, laid his hand on his shoulder, and whispered in his ear, "Get out of my class."

Familiar with the procedure, Stanley grabbed his coat and knapsack, and with the stomping of his feet, left the room. Thelma Lawson, the co-teacher in this eighth-grade, inclusive science class, ran after him. By the time she finally caught up to Stanley, he was angrily calling Mr. Gaskins a "mean old *$#!*."

"Stanley," said Mrs. Lawson as she put her hand on his shoulder, "you have to give it some effort if you hope to remain in mainstream science." Stanley wasn't certain that he wanted to remain in Gaskins's science class and, in fact, enjoyed last year when Mrs. Lawson taught him in her special education science.

"I learned so much from you," Stanley pleaded.

"I know that you did, but this year the principal has decided to change to collaborative teaching in inclusive classes. We're trying to get rid of segregated programs," Mrs. Lawson explained in return. "Look Stanley, let's think about what happened today," Mrs. Lawson counseled. "When you came into science class, you walked through the doors laughing, and then you slammed your bag down on the table. Next, you continued to talk to Sheena, even after the bell rang. Finally, halfway through Mr. Gaskins's introduction, you plopped your head down on the table and closed your eyes." Throughout Mrs. Lawson's analysis, Stanley stared at the ground, motionless, and said nothing. "Well, what do you think that you could have done differently?" she asked.

"The man is an old fool and his classes are boring," Stanley answered. Mrs. Lawson smiled at his response because she knew that, in part, his answer was correct.

Background Information

As she questioned Stanley's behavior, Mrs. Lawson knew that Mr. Gaskins was a very old-fashioned teacher who hated collaboration because it meant that the so-called "troubled kids" (i.e., those with learning disabilities, behavior disorders, and developmental disabilities) were now placed back in his class. Mr. Gaskins had worked hard to pass students with whom he was having problems to special education. Thelma saw Mr. Gaskins teach and felt sorry for the students. She knew that her hands were tied because, despite this being a collaborative class, her role was relegated to grading papers, assisting students, and helping Mr. Gaskins set up decades-old science experiments. Mr. Gaskins was quite open and honest with Thelma in telling her that he did not want to teach collaboratively and that he did not want those troubled kids in his class. He openly admitted to her that all that he wanted to do was do his job the way he knew how without any changes in his classroom.

For Thelma, who was new to the school, his attitude was far from what she wanted to hear. She had worked for the past three years in the elementary school, just minutes away, and was brought on board because the principal, John Makke, had been looking for someone in special education who could work with teachers like Mr. Gaskins. In fact, the running joke at Franklin Middle School was, "When is collaboration not collaboration? When you work with Mr. Gaskins." Thelma was a shining star at the elementary school, and her work in making the elementary school a collaborative environment had been the primary reason why John worked hard to recruit her for his school.

An inner-city school, Franklin City Middle School is located between an abandoned warehouse and the Guzzle and Go Liquor Store. It's not uncommon to see adults selling booze to underage youths who hang out near the store. For the youths, a few extra dollars to the adult usually secures their purchases. The high dropout rate in the district, which until recently mainly affected only the high school, was now being felt in the middle school. A lack of money for supplies and a lack of commitment from local officials meant that the future of the district was in jeopardy. Every election was full of promises by local politicians, yet every year the budget deficit became larger. The new gambling boats that were docked on the river to the east of the city were supposed to resolve the mounting deficit, but three years later the school district has yet to see much of the money that it was promised.

Mr. Gaskins' classroom is a pretty bland affair, far from a fountain of intellectual and emotional stimulation. The old gray walls have paint flaking off. The only color comes from a bulletin board that contains faded pictures of famous scientists. In the room, all 32 chairs are lined neatly in a row, with just barely enough room for even an adult to squeeze by. Mr. Gaskins's teaching is driven by the need to cover a specific amount of content material each week in order to cover the full sequence of annual achievement test items. Like other teachers, he has complained about the inordinate emphasis on achievement testing and how this emphasis has taken away teacher enthusiasm and thrown cold water on the magic moments when teachers finally make the connection with students—"the spark of learning," as he liked to call it.

Stanley, who despite being labeled behavior disordered (BD), was basically indistinguishable from the other students in the class; he was bored with the class and sick of school. Most of the students did not read the textbook or complete the countless worksheets that Mr. Gaskins required of his students. Mr. Gaskins called the students "lazy" and often blamed their lack of effort on their "deprived environment" rather than on his own teaching or curriculum.

For Stanley, his BD label was just that—a label. He had been identified BD three years ago following a solid 6 weeks of disruptive behavior. Despite his achievement in his classes, his excellent social skills, and his clean disciplinary record since that time, he remains categorized as BD. Stanley lives at home with his mother and older brother, Sharnel. Their parents have been divorced for 5 years, and often both children have expressed to their mother how difficult it is not to see their father. The divorce came about because of their father's continuous physical abuse of their mother. Having witnessed the beatings, both boys realize that it is probably better that they don't see their father for a while. Because Stanley's mother works the night shift at a local bar, the boys are on their own in the evenings. They often have to prepare for school on their own in the morning because their mother is usually sleeping. On this particular day, Stanley was sleepy because he was up all night watching TV and would have missed school if not for his brother.

CASE 7

DRIVIN' ME CRAZY

THE INCIDENT

When the screaming from the children in the back seat reached an ear-piercing crescendo, Lucinda pulled the car over to the shoulder on the highway, turned around, and yelled, "Tina! Stop hitting Elliot." This was the second time in the past 2 hours that Lucinda had pulled over and yelled at her kids. This time Tina hit Elliot because he wouldn't give her back her book. It was a long drive home for the children, who had just visited their grandparents. As Lucinda sat exasperated on the side of the highway with the motor idling, gusts from the trucks that passed by rocked the car. Lucinda continued to lecture the two children, telling them that she would "spank their bottoms" if she had to pull over again. She then grabbed the book from a tearful Elliot and tossed it to Tina. Lucinda turned on her left turn signal, crouched down to look out her side mirror, and pulled her 1972 Ford Fairlane back onto the busy highway.

Once back on the highway, Lucinda thought to herself about how badly her day had gone. "What a terrible way to leave their grandparents, with their mother arguing with their grandmother about how to raise children," Lucinda thought to herself. Within minutes, the children were again squabbling and poking at each other. Exiting into a gas station, Lucinda once again turned around and yelled at her children, even pleaded with them, to be quiet.

The scene just described is typical for Lucinda and her two children. Elliot and Tina often fight and yell at each other. The next morning, Lucinda talked with Tina's day care teacher, Mrs. Farrow, about these behavior problems. She told Mrs. Farrow the story about the miserable trip and asked for help. Mrs. Farrow listened carefully.

"Well, Lucinda," the teacher began, "it sounds like the kids need to learn to share toys." Unimpressed with this analysis of the situation, Tina looked at the teacher and remarked, "So what am I going to do?"

BACKGROUND INFORMATION

It had been 2 years since Lucinda's husband, Albert, had left her. Lucinda frequently commented that their 4 years of marriage had been "the worst 10 years" of her life. Albert is a chemical processing worker who was laid off by Blue Oil Company. He spent and continues to spend most of his days in the local bar drinking beer. He would usually start drinking around noon and continue well into the night. He would then return home, well after his family was asleep, and pass out in front of the television. Lucinda often suspected that Albert was having an affair but could never really prove it.

When her husband finally left, Lucinda realized that she now had the chance to lead the life that she wanted. For Albert, leaving his family meant a life without responsibility. Unfortunately for Lucinda, freedom came at a price. There would no longer be Albert's unemployment checks to support the family. Lucinda would have to get a full-time job, and she would have to place her children in the care of strangers at the local day care.

Lucinda blames the day care for her children's behavior problems. She often complains that once her children were placed in the day care, the problems at home began. At home, Tina, 4 years old, and Elliot, 2 years old, started to fight almost constantly. For example, one day as Lucinda was doing the wash, she heard young Elliot screaming from the next room. When she ran out to see what had happened, she found Elliot with a large red handprint on his back; the mark was from Tina's hand. She guessed that Elliot probably instigated this fight. Elliot often bugs his sister by taking her toys when she is playing with them and by repeating her name in a teasing singsong, over and over again. Lucinda realizes that Tina probably doesn't know how to handle Elliot's constant annoying behavior and has told Tina that if he bothers her, she should tell her mother. Despite her directions, the fighting continues and has become a way of life for the children. Similarly, yelling and spanking has become a habit for Lucinda. Even the neighbors in the apartment complex have complained about her shouting at her kids.

Lucinda's job at the meat processing factory requires that she work four 10-hour shifts per week. On those days, her children typically can spend up to 12 hours in day care. The job is taking a toll on Lucinda and her children to such an extent that she repeatedly complains to her boss about the long hours that she has to work. The boss has told her that the company has no flexibility in employee hours. Work the long shifts or lose the job.

On most days when Lucinda picks up her children at the day care, she is greeted at the door by a pretty frustrated day care teacher. Mrs. Farrow deals with many of the same problems that Lucinda deals with at home. Typically, the children are kept quite busy at the day care through a variety of activities such as playing group games, taking walks in the neighborhood, and watching videotapes. When problems arise, Mrs. Farrow typically resolves them by using a time-out chair. She sends the misbehaving child to a chair located in a solitary corner for 5 minutes. Then the child is invited to return to group activities. The chair has been effective most of the time for Elliot, but often has not worked with Tina. Sometimes she really doesn't seem to mind being sent to the chair. Other days she plops herself down on the floor and cries, refusing to budge an inch toward the chair. On those days, Mrs. Farrow calls Lucinda at work and asks her to talk to Tina on the telephone about her behavior. Lucinda typically threatens to punish Tina later on at home if she doesn't improve her behavior at day care. Lucinda's words seem to have little influence on Tina's unruly behavior.

Now at the end of her rope, Lucinda again asks Mrs. Farrow, "So what am I going to do?" Mrs. Farrow thinks seriously about what advice to give to Lucinda.

CASE 8

CRYING AND MARCHING

THE INCIDENT

Mr. Craig, a first-year teacher at Valley Trails Elementary School, looked briefly at little Zach Will and then nervously scanned the busy cafeteria. He quickly realized that there were no other teachers in this enormous room full of noisy children. He alone would have to deal with Zach, the fourth-grade boy who seemed to cry for at least 30 minutes every day. Zach was sitting alone at the end of a cafeteria bench, his fingers gently rolling a cold tater tot back and forth against the side of his face. The other children had cleared out, backed off, giving Zach space at the first sign of tears. Face bright red, tears rolling like the Mississippi during spring thaw, he was crying softly to himself.

As Mr. Craig walked hesitantly across the cafeteria toward Zach, he hardly noticed the rumbling din of 200 young children socializing over cheeseburgers and green jello. His mind rushed with images and thoughts from his own childhood. He recalled the day he went to see his father for the first time. He was 10 years old. His mother drove him up to the front gate of the property. He walked up and sat on the front porch with this strange and enormous man. They talked for 15 minutes, the distance between them growing more acute and glaring with each awkward word. Finally, little Billy Craig jumped off the porch and ran to the car where his mother waited. He cried all the way home, his head resting in her lap as she drove.

Suddenly, Mr. Craig recalled the staff meeting in which his principal, Mrs. Debaliviere, outlined the plan for dealing with Zach Will's frequent episodes of crying.

"That crying behavior is pure manipulation," Mrs. Debaliviere had explained. "He wants attention and has to learn not to seek it in a negative way. When he exhibits the crying behavior, wherever that may be, simply and firmly march him down to my office."

Looking up, Mr. Craig realized that he had arrived. He had walked across the cafeteria and was now standing 2 feet from 9-year-old Zach. Zach's tears were still flowing.

"Let's go, Zach," Mr. Craig heard himself saying in a surprisingly sharp tone. "You know the drill. Down to the office. Let's march." Zach walked peaceably with the teacher to the office, tears running fully with every step. At the boy's side marched Mr. Craig. His powerful sense of discomfort about punishing a boy for crying raged silently as he simply did his professional duty.

Background Information

Much vital insight into this situation may be gleaned from a glimpse into the vocalized words and silent thoughts of the various professionals who attended the staff meeting concerning Zach. At that meeting, held a week before the above incident, Mrs. Debaliviere detailed the intervention plan calling for teachers to "march" this crying youngster to the office.

When Mrs. Debaliviere holds a staff meeting, she directs the discussion with a no-nonsense attitude and one eye on her wristwatch. She hands out an agenda of discussion items to the teachers. Next to each item is an incremental time allotment, typically between 2 and 5 minutes per topic. Principal Debaliviere tends to talk about each item for most of the time allotment. When she opens up an item for discussion, the teachers are generally silent. They simply await her decision on the matter.

Ms. Normandy, Zach's third-grade teacher, was surprised to see *Zach Will's crying* listed as the third agenda item for that October 19 staff meeting. After quickly moving through two minor issues concerning bus duty and the upcoming visit by the regional assistant superintendent, Mrs. Debaliviere addressed item 3, a 2-minute item.

"Agenda item number 3, a disciplinary item. Zachary Will of Ms. Normandy's class has had 10 extended crying jags over the course of 3 weeks. These episodes have been lasting over 30 minutes. Three have occurred in Ms. Normandy's classroom, five in the cafeteria, one in the front hallway, one in Mr. Edelson's music class. I've seen this sort of thing before, one student drawing the attention of the teacher in a negative way and thereby disrupting the learning process for others. Some of you may recall a little girl in Mrs. Beezeley's room a few years back. Eunice, who was that girl?"

"Her name was Wendy Watkins," replied Eunice Beezeley, a veteran teacher. "She cried every day for a week, if I recall correctly."

"Yes, Eunice, that's the one," Principal Debaliviere continued. "Wendy Watkins would go on for an hour. We instituted a plan whereby Mrs. Beezeley sent Wendy to the office at the first sign of a tear. It was crucial not to wait on this behavior. Mrs. Beezeley intervened quickly, brought the child to my office, and I set her in a time-out chair in the corner behind the large filing cabinet. The child only needed to be sent to me twice and the problem was solved."

As Mrs. Debaliviere recalled this experience from the past and then briefly detailed the plan for all teachers to implement the same intervention with Zach Will, the teachers of Valley Trails Elementary School listened silently. Behind their silence stirred much information and insight concerning this situation. The thoughts of Mrs. Beezeley, Ms. Ellis, and Mr. Craig provide us with much information about this problem of Zach's crying.

Mrs. Beezeley wondered why little Zach was crying. She recalled that many months after the intervention that effectively halted Wendy Watkins's crying bouts, she had bumped into Wendy's mother at the supermarket. Wendy's mother thanked Mrs. Beezeley for teaching Wendy to truly love reading. As Eunice Beezeley felt the sweet glow of satisfaction, Mrs. Watkins went on to explain how reading had been a source of tremendous solace to Wendy after the death of her grandfather. Mrs. Beezeley recalled that she had asked tear-flushed Wendy over and over, "What's wrong? Why are you crying?" But Wendy had never explained. She just blubbered on and on. Mrs. Beezeley wished she had known about her grandfather's death much earlier.

Ms. Ellis, the school guidance counselor, recalled that she had almost met with Zach's mother this past spring. There had been a class field trip to the aquarium, and Zach had forgotten to return his permission slip. Ms. Ellis had called simply to ask Zach's mother if her boy could go on the trip. Little Zach sat in the beanbag chair across from the guidance counselor, eyes downcast at the thought of not going on the trip. He hadn't cried at all, Ms. Ellis recalled. Zach's mother approved the field trip and asked to meet with Ms. Ellis to discuss some difficulties she was having with Zach at home. Apparently, Zach's father had moved out, and a new boyfriend had moved in, stirring some issues and misbehavior on Zach's part. From the anxious tone in the mother's voice, Ms. Ellis interpreted that there was much more to the story than a boy having trouble adjusting to a new father figure. Ms. Ellis recalled setting up a meeting to discuss the problem, but Zach's mother hadn't showed up. When she subsequently didn't return three of Ms. Ellis's phone calls, the counselor had allowed the issue to drop.

Mr. Craig, an eager new teacher, spent the meeting diligently recording Principal Debaliviere's directions in his notebook. As the principal described the problem of Zach Will's crying, Mr. Craig pictured himself sitting down next to the lad on the floor, consoling the evidently sad youngster. This was the type of caring that Mr. Craig had hoped to bring to children by becoming a teacher. Then he noticed that his principal spoke about problems and solutions with an incredible degree of self-assurance. She seemed to immediately know exactly what to do in each situation. Her voice and demeanor were filled with the kind of confidence that he knew he lacked. He thought about his professional struggle to become more of a firm authority with the children. His first month of teaching had been a nightmare. He offered continuous kindness and his class of fifth graders walked all over him. Mrs. Debaliviere and the other teachers began coaching him to "get tough" and "lay down the law." Since then, he has been trying to strike some sort of balance between kindness and authority, caring and power. Before he could fully consider this dilemma, Mr. Craig's attention was broken by the principal's voice.

"Agenda item number 4, the implementation of a new science curriculum."

CASE 9

DEMOLITION DAN

THE INCIDENT

"Boom! Boom!" shouted Danny as he jumped up and down. His small frame quivered with excitement. At his feet lay a pile of blocks that Caitlin had previously stacked neatly in the shape of a house. When Caitlin looked up from the water fountain, she let out a loud scream. Meanwhile Danny just kept repeating "Boom, boom, boom" as he ran to Cynthia's play area.

Using her arms as a shield to protect her block building, little Cynthia shouted at him, "No Danny! No! No!" It was too late; her building came crashing to the ground. Danny stood over it jumping up and down, screaming "Boom! Boom!" By the time Eileen Hattson had grabbed Danny's arm, he was already on his way to another play site, with the possibility of destroying another child's block building.

"Danny, you do not destroy other kids' blocks," Eileen told the boy as she bent down to look at him at eye level. But Danny, uninterested in listening to another lecture about "appropriate" behavior, looked away and continued jumping up and down. "Look at me! Look at me!" Eileen insisted. She then took him by the hand, walked over to Caitlin's pile of blocks, and requested that Danny help her build a new house. "Think about what you did and how sad you made Caitlin feel," lectured Eileen. "You need to learn to not destroy other children's work," she reiterated as she sat him on her lap in front of the blocks.

BACKGROUND INFORMATION

Immediately prior to the above incident, Danny became angry on the playground. Coming in from recess, Danny was still quite angry about the incident that occurred outside. On the playground, Danny was teased by two older children who thought his little body and large head looked odd. They began calling him names, and he responded by kicking their toys. He was still kicking when Eileen grabbed him by the arm and helped him inside the school. Once inside, Eileen got the children involved in activities on small carpet squares. Each child was expected to play on a carpet square for only 10 minutes before he or she moved on to the next activity. After another 10 minutes, like clockwork, each child moved to another carpet square.

Currently, Danny is enrolled in Mrs. Hattson's preschool class, a program affiliated with Ocean Mist University. The Ocean Mist Preschool is run by Dorothy Perkins, a graduate of Ocean Mist, who utilizes a constructivist approach to classroom management. For Danny this means that the solutions to his behavioral problems occur by helping him to gain a more active understanding of his actions and how those actions affect others. Mrs. Perkins believes that it only through a more active self-understanding of a child's actions that each child can understand the social and moral value of those actions and be more willing to possibly change his or her behavior. For most children, this constructivist approach has led to a successful resolution of their inappropriate behaviors; for others, many of their actions continue to cause social unrest among their classmates.

Although Danny has been labeled developmentally delayed in the areas of social competence and language skills, he has managed to fit in well with his classmates—some of whom have disabilities. The 12 students in the class, as a group, have functioned well in their cooperative learning environment. Over the past 3 months, Eileen has taught the students to develop a buddy system for both play and learning. Students are teamed in duos and taught to help and look out for the well-being of their buddies. Buddies are exchanged on a periodic basis to give children experiences playing and learning with different peers. Now in her second year of teaching, Eileen has enjoyed working with the variety of students who come from different and varied cultures. On the whole, she has done well at teaching her students appropriate educational and social skills, but Danny continually gives her problems with his "destructive" nature.

Nicknamed "Demolition Dan" by his teacher, Danny often gets into confrontations with other students and frequently destroys their projects (i.e., artwork, toys, and worksheets). Danny loves to tear paper. Eileen has learned that she needs to keep all paper products out of Danny's sight. On one recent occasion, when she left Danny alone in the room for a few minutes, she returned to confetti-like pieces of her newspaper spread out on the floor. After making Danny clean up the mess, she decided to never again leave him unattended. This pattern of destroying objects has occurred at other times as well. For example, a few days ago, Danny managed to sneak Anthony's show-and-tell project, a tape recorder, from his desk and, within 30 seconds, had it smashed in pieces on the ground.

Danny currently lives with foster parents, Lucy and Hank Contor, and six other foster children. Lucy and Hank have had similar problems with Danny at home. For instance, Hank recently told Eileen that when Danny wanted a milkshake, he crawled up on the counter, grabbed the blender, and threw it on the floor. In the past, Hank had used the blender to make homemade milkshakes for the kids. It is now broken, and a gate at the entrance to their kitchen keeps Danny from possibly damaging the other kitchen appliances. In addition to his indoor escapades, Danny has also wreaked a fair amount of havoc outside the Contor household. A few weeks ago when Danny was playing outside, he somehow crawled under the fence to the garden. When Lucy noticed that he was missing, she called Hank and a search of the family property ensued. After 10 minutes, Lucy found Danny hidden behind the tomato plants, tearing out the plants by their roots.

In teacher-parent conferences, both Eileen and Lucy agree that Danny needs to work on his destructiveness and his language problems. For a 3-year old, Danny communicates with a limited number of vocabulary words. Often Danny is able to make his requests known through grunts or a small repertoire of words and hand gestures. His language skills are believed to be delayed for reasons both neurological and social. It seems that his neurological development is slow in language areas. Also, it is possible that his foster family supports his lack of language use. His six siblings are always around to assist Danny and eagerly get him whatever he wants, thereby reducing his need to communicate with words. Usually, Danny has appropriate interactions with his siblings until his destructive actions cause problems. Realizing that someday Danny will be leaving, his temporary family do their best to deal with him.

CASE 10

DEPEND ON ME

THE INCIDENT

A small squabble was brewing between two 3-year-olds in the bright yellow sandbox area in the corner of the classroom. As Sandy Brown attempted to walk across her classroom to deal with the problem, her right leg dragged as if it were attached to a large sack of flour. She smiled at her friend Felix Gassoway, a university classmate and observer in her class. She pointed at her dragging leg and mouthed the word *Jason*. Felix, knowing full well to whom she was referring, twisted his head sideways and furrowed his brow, as if to say, "Jason? What Jason? I don't see any Jason." Sandy shot Felix a mock scowl and limped as quickly as possible toward the mini-battle stewing in the sandbox. Jason hung on tight for every step.

Felix and Sandy were graduate students collaborating on an action research project for a special education course at a nearby university. One morning per week, Felix observed in Sandy's class and took extensive field notes on behavior problems. Sandy read his weekly reports and wrote back her own observations and thoughts concerning behavior problems in her classroom.

As Sandy walked past Felix, the body of a small boy clinging desperately to the teacher's leg became visible. He was losing his grip on her slacks, sliding down, and mumbling a list of preverbal demands. Finally, Sandy scooped the boy up with her hand and pulled him up to the relative safety of her hip. Felix watched Sandy tote this youngster around as she taught the other children for the next half hour, then he jotted this down in his observational field notes: "The boy must be four years old. He is much too large to be carried around like an infant. Yet he repeatedly demands that Ms. Brown carry him. Very dependent. Can this dependency be decreased? Is Ms. Brown only nurturing this dependency by holding him so much? And how does this affect the other children? Last question: Why is the paraprofessional sitting at her desk while Ms. Brown is running from needy child to needy child?"

BACKGROUND INFORMATION

Sandy Brown is a second-year teacher at the Alliance Preschool, a program that fully includes youngsters with disabilities or developmental delays with their typical age peers. Her classroom paraprofessional is Ella Williamson, a 14-year veteran of various special education classrooms throughout the district. This is her fifth year in the inclusive preschool program.

Jason is a 4-year-old boy who was adopted 2 years ago from an orphanage in Romania. His adoptive parents saw a program on television showing the atrocious, overcrowded conditions in many Romanian orphanages and decided to save one child from that terrible fate. Jason undoubtedly bears the emotional scars of an infancy spent in an institution lacking clean water, healthy food, and adequate loving contact with adults. He has additional developmental delays that may be unrelated to the poor care he received as a baby. His speech is loud but very difficult to understand. He speaks a repertoire of about 20 words. His listening comprehension is far more advanced, close to that of age peers. Additionally, he seems to have a neurological impairment that cannot yet be clearly diagnosed. His gross motor functioning is similar to age peers, but his fine motor skills are significantly delayed. His hands and arms are weak and poorly coordinated. He has tremendous difficulty holding a crayon or scooping up sand with a spoon. At times, Jason has displayed behaviors typical of autism; specifically, Jason has held his hands up between his eyes and the overhead lights, fixating visually on the play of light across the motion of his fingers. Sometimes he has sat off by himself, rocking his body and repeating a single word or phrase for 15 to 20 minutes.

Socially, Jason tends to have little interest in his peers. He is able to play or learn in a small group of children, but his attention inevitably zeroes in on an adult. Generally, with an occasional exception when Ella will hold Jason at her desk, Jason has sought out Sandy's affection. Sandy has been baffled about what to do. She finds herself literally carrying Jason around for half of her time. She has tried setting him down and directing him to play with a favorite toy or work on an activity, but this has frequently brought on a crying bout or a spell of body rocking and verbal rumination. With Ella's encouragement ("You must break him of this nonsense"), Sandy once allowed Jason to cry for over 40 minutes before she finally returned to scoop him up and dry his eyes. He just doesn't seem able to get along without her.

Sandy asked her university classmate Felix to observe closely and try to offer some solutions for handling Jason. By reading Felix's notes, Sandy has learned that she carries Jason around much more than she realized. It is not uncommon that Sandy organizes and leads the other children in a group activity such as singing a song while holding Jason on her hip. Like a habitual smoker who notices the cigarette in her mouth but does not recall lighting one up, Sandy carries Jason around without even noticing what she is doing.

Although Sandy originally directed Felix to concentrate his observations on her difficulties with Jason, Felix's notes soon shifted to something he found equally interesting—that is, the way that Ella remained at her desk at the front of the classroom for hours at a time, interacting very little with the children. In reading Felix's notes, Sandy soon realized that she was doing 80% to 90% of the direct work with the children while Ella remained very distant and uninvolved. If a child specifically went to Ella, she would respond and play with the child. But Ella rarely initiated interaction with the youngsters. Sandy admitted to Felix that as a young teacher she felt like she had entered into a classroom owned by Ella. Although she is officially Ella's supervisor, she has felt little authority in critiquing and correcting her older colleague's work habits.

By the end of the semester, Felix had begun to write small interpretations and questions that brought together the two problems (i.e., Jason's dependency and Ella's lack of involvement with the students). He noted that some of the other children seemed to resent Jason for monopolizing their teacher's affections. At times, he connected the angry or sad moods of certain youngsters to their inability to gain access to their teacher's love and attention. Felix wondered if this situation couldn't be alleviated by the active participation of one other adult, namely Ella. How would the active involvement of that one adult help to satisfy the needs for nurturing and affection that were so obvious in Jason and quite evident in the other children?

After talking to Felix about Ella's lack of involvment with the students, Sandy decided to seek the advice of the director of the Alliance Preschool, Dr. Amy Chu. Dr. Chu had been a professor of child development at Eastern State University before she decided to leave academic work to found Alliance, an experimental preschool program in a major city. The program consists of a staff of four certified teachers and four teacher aides, supplemented by a number of parent volunteers. A total of 55 youngsters between the ages of 3 and 5 are served.

The Alliance Preschool, now 5 years old, is located in an old plastics factory building within easy walking distance from the low-income housing apartments where over a thousand families live. Soon after the doors opened that first August, the professionals found themselves working side by side with a small but dedicated group of parent volunteers from the neighborhood. Most of the volunteers are mothers in their late teens who left high school to have children. Those volunteers founded a small GED study program on the Alliance site in the evenings. Sandy has taught some of the classes designed to help the parents earn their GEDs and move on to community college or vocational programs.

Many local educators, Sandy included, consider Dr. Chu to be something of a visionary in the field of early childhood education. Dr. Chu openly rejects the common language-based approach utilized in many preschools that serve urban children of color. She believes adamantly that these predominantly African-American and Hispanic children do not require a constant message that their spoken dialect is "wrong" and in need of correction. In her oft-repeated words: "How could a child who is told daily that her words are wrong in comparison with an abstraction called 'standard English' develop any self-esteem?" Instead, Dr. Chu has developed an exploratory arts-based program in which the youngsters are given opportunities to produce aesthetic and cultural symbols such as drawings, paintings, and clay figures.

The teachers of Alliance share Dr. Chu's vision, but they also find their director to be a difficult person to approach with everyday problems. In some ways, Dr. Chu tends to be a hands-off administrator. She handles the budget, makes a number of high-profile speaking engagements promoting the school and raising funds throughout the state, and works closely with her teachers on the development of the arts-based curriculum. When it comes to mundane matters involving conflicts between adults, Dr. Chu seems either to not care or simply to not know what to do.

With a fair amount of hesitancy, Sandy approached her supervisor with her issue regarding Ella Williamson. She explained Felix's observations and her desire that Ella get out from behind her desk and be active with the children. Dr. Chu listened carefully and assured Sandy that she would talk to Ella about this issue without letting on that Sandy had complained. As she walked out of the director's office, Sandy felt relieved and hopeful.

For the next 3 weeks, Sandy saw a marked improvement in Ella's work. She played with the children and even toted Jason for up to a half hour at a time. It even seemed that she might be able to teach Jason a little independence. She would carry him for a while, then set him down and play with him, gradually creating some distance between herself and this very dependent toddler. After the 3 good weeks, however, Sandy noticed Ella slipping back into her old habits, sitting behind her desk instead of participating among the students.

CASE **11**

CRASHING PLANES AND TRANQUIL DREAMS

THE INCIDENT

As nap time approached, Sandy Werton knew it was going to be another rough day because Richard had arrived at school more active than ever. "That boy has more energy than I ever had at his age," Sandy commented to Jill Bosco, the aide in the class. Sandy looked at her watch and announced to her class, "Well, it's 12 o'clock. Nap time." With her comment, the six students in her class let out a chorus of moans. At the time, most students were busy playing with their toys, except for Richard, who was running around the room pretending to be an airplane. Within a few minutes, the students were nestled down on their mats with small white blankets covering them, except for Richard, who was practicing "emergency landing" procedures, accompanied by screeching noises to simulate the twisting metal of a plane crash.

"Richard, this is the second time I've had to tell you to get over here to lie down," Sandy spoke in a low but firm voice. Richard, oblivious to anything but the plane wreck, continued to play. Sandy, moving closer to him, again spoke, "Richard, get yourself over here and lie down."

This time Richard looked up and, realizing that he was the only one not lying down, cried out, "I don't wanna nap now. I no tired now." To these responses, Sandy lifted him up and carried his small but wiry body over to his mat.

"Look Richard, you need to sleep. Every day we go over this. It is time for your nap. Now, let's go. Get to sleep!" explained Sandy in a hushed voice. She set him down gently on his mat. As soon as Sandy walked away from Richard, he got up, began making airplane noises, and ran toward his toy plane sitting on the shelf. For Sandy, this battle with Richard was an almost daily occurrence.

BACKGROUND INFORMATION

Richard finally fell asleep. It took Sandy 20 minutes to get him settled and quiet. After many threats, yelling, and tears (Richard's), he finally closed his eyes. Although the quiet room is a respite for Sandy, it does not last long. Ten minutes later, Richard is awake giggling and laughing. Sandy calls over to him to be quiet, but she knows that he is awake for the rest of the school day. Jill, now back from lunch, sees Richard awake and runs over to quiet him down. After a few fruitless minutes, she directs him to some toys in the box. Meanwhile, Sandy is busy writing notes to send home. Again, Sandy has to report that Richard did not sleep very long and that there was an incident in the bathroom, in which Richard had thrown a cup of water on another student. As Sandy writes the note for Richard's parents, she again contemplates how best to handle Richard. She has tried to get him to nap by taking away his recess, taking away his snack, and threatening to call his parents but has had no luck. The director of the program has suggested that she use stickers or candy to reinforce his behavior on those days when he follows the rules, but Sandy feels that this would not be fair to the rest of the class.

Richard, now 4 years old, has been in the YMCA's full-day preschool program for the past 2 years. Richard gets along fairly well with other students, although his parents and teachers often comment about his "hyper" behavior. They suspect that he might have an attention deficit disorder, but he has yet to be formally diagnosed. Aside from his "hyper" behavior, impulsiveness, and an occasional battle with adults, Richard is generally thought of as a "good" kid who occasionally gets into trouble. He is bright and well liked by the other children and adults. He often surprises adults with pictures drawn for them, along with words of "I love you." His sweet smile and funny facial expressions often negate any bad news that he brings home.

Richard lives at home with two brothers, Zarell and David, aged 9 and 10. His parents, Tom and Latisha Green, realize that Richard is, at times, overly active, but they often blame his hyperactivity on excessive sweets or drinks. Tom does not spend a lot of time at home. He has a busy schedule that includes a lot of overtime work, needed to help pay the bills, and a number of commitments with the church and local little league. When Tom does spend time with Richard, he usually ends up yelling at him or sending him to his room for getting into things that he shouldn't have gotten into (e.g., Tom's tool box, the birdseed, or the trash). Because of Tom and Latisha's religious convictions, they spend a lot of time in church or involved in church-related activities. Church is another setting where Richard frequently gets in trouble. He is constantly out of his seat, and sometimes he inadvertently makes noises. These behaviors have embarrassed the parents on a number of occasions and resulted in Richard being taken outside to receive a spanking.

Because child care at the YMCA is expensive, Latisha often works long hours, resulting in 10 to 12 hour days at preschool (including the before- and after-school program) for Richard. Latisha regrets working long hours and often considers quitting the "rat race" for shorter days and more quality time with her children. Latisha has left work on more than one occasion to attend to her children's needs at school and home. Her busy schedule frequently keeps her from enjoying life with her kids, but the difficult reality of a two-person working family holds true for the Greens.

Zarell, Richard's older brother, has a quick temper and tends to get in fights at school. About one day per month, Latisha receives a phone call from Zarell's school—because he has gotten into another fight. Latisha tells her boss and dashes off to school to pick up Zarell. As she drives to school, she wonders how Richard is doing and contemplates how many future trips she will have to make to one of her sons' schools to resolve problems.

At home, Richard gets yelled at quite a few times during the evening because, as Latisha states, "he just doesn't listen sometimes." Latisha and Tom use yelling and "the chair" (time-out) as their forms of management, and these methods seem to work well. For example, last evening Richard did not eat all of his dinner; actually, he only ate a few bites of food. Even before finishing his meal, he asked Latisha for a candy bar. When she refused to give one to him, Richard threw himself on the floor and began kicking and crying. Latisha yelled at him to stop and threatened to put him on "the chair." Then, realizing that she doesn't spend much time with him, she gave in and handed him the candy bar. This pattern of behavior and response is common for the two; that is, he yells, she threatens, and then she gives in. By the time Tom arrives home, typically around 8 o'clock, any problems that have arisen are resolved. Usually, Richard is asleep in his bed, and the other two boys are wrestling on the floor while the TV plays in the background.

CASE 12

PULLED AT THE EDGES

THE INCIDENT

Eric looked across the bus at the box of bag lunches. He suddenly realized that there would be no hot lunch served in the cafeteria today, that bag lunches consisting of sandwiches had been packed instead. He started crying. By the time the small yellow bus carrying Mrs. Stevens's class was driving down Interstate 95, Eric's tears had escalated up to a full howl.

"Oh, I should have seen this one coming," groaned Mr. Edwards, the classroom aide.

Mrs. Stevens smiled and shrugged her shoulders. "Par for the course," she said with a tone of resignation.

Mr. Edwards turned to Eric. "Come on, Eric, you ate a bologna sandwich last week. Remember? I put the spicy mustard on it for you." Mr. Edwards tried to calm Eric down. Noticing that Eric seemed to take some pleasure in remembering the mustard, Mr. Edwards repeated the phrase *spreading the mustard* while pretending to spread mustard along the top of Eric's hand. This gradually soothed Eric and turned into a friendly little game with Mr. Edwards rubbing Eric's hand.

By the time Mr. Edward got Eric settled down, Irving's whining had escalated into screaming and bouncing in his seat. He kept pointing at Sara. The bus had pulled up to the curb in front of the Overland Mall. Mrs. Stevens rushed across the aisle to find out what was happening. Sara was bleeding from a wound at the edge of her mouth. As she pulled at the corner of her mouth with her index finger, the cut widened and more blood rushed down the side of her face. Irving, the child seated in his wheelchair next to Sara, was frightened by the sight of blood. He was screaming at the top of his lungs. The five other students, all middle schoolers categorized as having moderate and severe levels of developmental disabilities, were becoming increasingly distressed by the commotion.

BACKGROUND INFORMATION

Sara is a 13-year-old girl with cerebral palsy. School records describe her as functioning intellectually within the severe range of developmental disability. In the past 6 months, she has been noted to exhibit some autistic behaviors. She does not speak in words, although she understands a variety of words spoken to her. At school, she tends to isolate herself and not notice people and events in her immediate environment. She engages in behaviors that the staff calls "self-stimulatory," mainly poking and squeezing her cheeks with her fingers. The mildest form of this involves repetitive tapping on the hollows of her cheeks, as if she were producing a drum beat. In the most severe form of this behavior, Sara places her fingers under her lips at the corner of her mouth and yanks repeatedly. This has often caused the edge of her mouth to become red or inflamed or split wide open. At the time of this incident, the edges of Sara's mouth were encrusted with large scabs.

Concerned with the frequency and severity of Sara's self-injurious behavior, Mrs. Stevens and Mr. Edwards conducted a brief functional analysis. For 1 week, they observed Sara very closely. For each of the instances when she tugged on her lip with her fingers, they wrote down the contextual factors present immediately before and after the behavior. These factors included environmental conditions such as learning activities, interactions with peers or adults, and interactions with stimulating or interesting objects. The purpose of this analysis was to figure out what specific environmental conditions seem to support or provoke Sara's behavior. Mrs. Stevens and Mr. Edwards found that Sara tended to grab her lip when she became upset or anxious. This anxiety could be triggered by many kinds of stimuli, but often the behavior immediately followed episodes of loud and dramatic behavior by Eric. Sara and Eric had been classmates in special programs together since the first day each entered public school. Though they rarely played together, Sara was particularly tuned to Eric's emotions and behavior. When he was upset or agitated, Sara was likely to follow.

Based on this knowledge, Sara's teachers tried two specific strategies to reduce Sara's self-injurious behavior. First, they organized learning activities in such a way as to often keep Sara and Eric physically separated. That way, if Eric became upset, Sara might not even know. His influence would be diminished by distance. Second, they analyzed and addressed the kinds of situations and conditions that tended to upset Eric. The teachers reasoned that if they could learn to keep Eric settled down, that calm would help Sara, too. The incident detailed above occurred on the third day of the implementation of these new strategies.

For the past 2 years, Sara has lived at the Weldon Home, a small foster care facility for children with special needs. The decision to place her at Weldon was very difficult for her parents. They held a strong belief that Sara belonged at home with her family. But her behavior had deteriorated.

She sometimes flew into wild tantrums, breaking toys and furniture, sometimes injuring herself in the process. She was growing too large for her mother, grandmother, and sister to physically control. Due to Sara's increasingly difficult behavior at home, the family had little choice but to seek outside support. They were saddened to find that hiring qualified caregivers to assist in their home was beyond their financial means. An out-of-home placement was their only alternative.

After an extensive search into local placement options, Sara's parents settled on the Weldon Home, a facility that houses eight school-aged girls with developmental disabilities and autism. The staff is knowledgeable and caring. It is unfortunately located 52 miles away from their home. This makes family visits during the week very difficult. Also, Sara had to change schools, shifting from the special school for students with severe disabilities that she had attended for many years to Mrs. Stevens's self-contained classroom at a middle school near the Weldon Home.

For many years, her parents and her younger sister had enjoyed Sara's company in their home. The family enjoyed weekends at the lake with Sara's grandparents. As a young child, Sara always enjoyed riding in the family motorboat. She also had a special connection to her grandmother. There were some days when the entire family would run off to go fishing and swimming, leaving young Sara curled up in her grandmother's arms and listening to stories. When the family returned for dinner, they'd find Sara and her grandmother in that same spot on the wicker couch with an old army blanket tossed across the two to hold off the evening chill.

Over the past year, Sara's grandmother has become ill. Due to her weakened condition, she is unable to drive to the Weldon Home to visit her granddaughter. Since Sara comes home every weekend, the two are able to spend some time together about once or twice each month. During these visits, Sara has thrown tantrums when she has not been allowed to curl up in her grandmother's lap. She doesn't understand that she has grown too large and her grandmother has become too weak to hold her.

Sara's teacher is Mrs. Stevens, a young, somewhat idealistic first-year special education teacher. She has dramatically changed the curriculum of this class to involve the students more in community activities. The tradition has been to keep students with severe mental disabilities in their classroom at the far west wing of Callahan Middle School. Mrs. Stevens has surprised her principal by taking her students into the community once or twice each week. While her principal has expressed some ambivalence about "shaking things up unnecessarily," he also has arranged for bus transportation for these trips. In the past 2 weeks, however, he has received three phone calls from concerned parents of students in Mrs. Stevens's class who claim that the trips into the community have somehow caused their children to have increased instances of misbehavior at home.

Mr. Edwards is an elderly gentleman who has been a special education classroom aide for 26 years. Mrs. Stevens is the third teacher he has worked with in his 9 years in the self-contained class at Callahan Middle School. He considers himself to be the backbone of the program, the one constant in this classroom over the years. He has seen a number of educational fads come and go. He is skeptical about Mrs. Stevens's enthusiasm for bringing the students into the community. He would rather protect them from failure and the staring eyes of the public by remaining within the classroom. Additionally, Mr. Edwards claims that the community trips only reduce the structure and routine of the program, thereby increasing the negative behavior of the students.

Sara's class consists of seven students who are categorized as having moderate to severe developmental disabilities. The students range in age from 12 to 15 years old. There are five boys and two girls. Sara is one of four students in the class who do not speak. The other three students vary in their oral language skills.

CASE 13

FIFTEEN SECONDS OF FAME

THE INCIDENT

As Henry Hennison looked down the hallway, his eyes lit up in amazement. Blowing up and down on the hallway walls were pieces of paper that represented each child's artwork, homework, or special project. All day long as students walked down the center of the hallway, papers taped to the walls on both sides blew at them in every direction. It was actually a stimulating tactile experience as the sides of their bodies were gently touched by paper or paper products. As in most schools, the papers or projects from every classroom that hung outside each room were chosen to showcase each child's best work. On this particular hot, windy day, each classroom had its windows and doors open, creating a "wind tunnel" effect in the hall. The cool breeze felt good on the tired brows of the countless children who made trips to the bathroom located at the far end of the hall.

With the hall now empty, Henry suddenly had an enlightened idea. Backing up to the outside doors, Henry announced his ambitious intentions with the words, "Ready, set, go." He then took off at full speed down the hallway with his arms stretched wide, grabbing as many papers off the walls as he could. In his tracks lay the remains of his "drag race": ripped papers spread all over the hallway floor. When he neared the end of the hallway, a pair of large hands reached out from nowhere to grab him by the shirt collar and reel him in from his pillaging run. The hands belonged to none other than Mr. George Dillard, the school principal. Looking down the messy hallway, Mr. Dillard's lower jaw dropped, and his voice trembled with anger. "What are you doing?" hollered Mr. Dillard. Before Henry could answer, Mr. Dillard shouted again, "What in the world have you done?" Realizing that his 15-second fantasy drag race had landed him in the hands of an angry principal, Henry began to cry uncontrollably. With tears rolling down his small face, he realized that his impulsiveness had again gotten him in trouble. Meanwhile, down the hall, curious students poked their heads out into the hallway to see what had happened.

BACKGROUND INFORMATION

Some temptations in life are just too good to pass by. Unfortunately, for Henry many temptations in life were too good to pass by. Although he was only 7 years old, Henry's impulsiveness has gotten him into more predicaments than most children twice his age. *Immature, out of control,* and *wild* are the words that he has heard over and over again to describe him and his behavior. Yesterday, his teacher scolded him for banging on the computer keyboard as the other children were typing in information. Two days ago, he shifted the car gears from park to drive when his mother, Yolanda, stepped out of the vehicle to put a package in the trunk. Jerking forward, the car rolled 10 yards and plowed into the garage door. Last Saturday, he almost electrocuted himself after he stuck a fork into the videotape player when his *Toy Story* videotape wouldn't eject. Last week, Henry pushed his classmate, Lucy, down the steps when she suddenly stopped in front of him. Henry claimed it was an "accident."

Henry has had many such "accidents" in his life. Yolanda often remarks that she "could write a book" about Henry's trials and tribulations. Almost daily Yolanda hears from his teacher, a neighbor, or other children about Henry's latest destructive or dangerous acts. For her, no news is the best news. Yolanda feels that Henry is a "good-hearted" child who does not really mean to harm other people or break things. Consequently, when Henry does get into trouble, Yolanda calmly talks to him about the incident, tells him to be "more careful next time," and then sends him back to whatever he was doing. It is only on rare occasions that Yolanda sends Henry to his room for his accidents. Yolanda also feels that Henry sometimes "acts up" because he is having trouble dealing with her separation from his father, Harry.

With Henry's latest incident, the hallway drag race, Mr. Dillard sent him to see the school counselor, Ms. Carrie Anthan. Ms. Anthan has seen Henry on a weekly to twice-weekly basis. Her file on Henry describes a troubled child who often seeks attention through inappropriate actions. In personal counseling sessions with her, Henry has told Ms. Anthan of his racing thoughts and lack of control in turning thoughts into actions. She feels that Henry is actually depressed and often acts out in reaction to his sad thoughts. She has tried a number of interventions with him including substituting positive for negative thoughts and counting to 10 before reacting to irrational thoughts, a lot of "heavy stuff" for a 7-year-old. In reaction to some of her more complex suggestions, Henry once blurted out, "I'm only 7 years old." Although Ms. Anthan and Yolanda have spoken about Henry's behavior and possible remedies, Yolanda often dismisses her suggestions as "psychological mumbo jumbo" and Henry's actions as those of a typical 7-year-old.

Henry's father, whom the boy sees on weekends, also has to deal with many of the same inappropriate actions. The difference is that Harry deals differently with little Henry's behavior. Harry's approach to dealing with Henry involves slapping him on the buttocks. This method of discipline usually works out well for Harry, and in the short run, Henry behaves. Henry respects and, at times, fears his father. Henry has talked to Yolanda about his fear of his father and his reluctance to visit him. However, when Yolanda spoke to Harry about Henry's fears, Harry dismissed it as the foolish talk of a child and even told Yolanda that she should try being stern with Henry to help him control his behavior. Despite Henry's improved behavior after a spanking, it doesn't take him long before he is again in trouble with his father.

CASE 14

WHEN FEAR RULES THE LAND

THE INCIDENT

While the shrieks of joy were heard from children playing games on the front playground, behind the school a very different story was unfolding. Off in a quiet area behind a row of thick shrubs came a "thump" followed by the muted sounds of a young child crying. It was Maryjo Hanley beating up a smaller child who had challenged her authority. "Next time I want to copy your homework you better let me or else you'll get more of this," whispered Maryjo into the ear of her latest victim, Fran Klenck. Maryjo and her two sidekicks, Leeanne and Shirley, released Fran from their grip.

Fran, with an ache in her stomach and tears streaming down her cheeks, ran to a vacant corner of the playground and hid her face in shame. Her mind wandered back to last week. On Monday, she had volunteered her spelling homework for Maryjo to copy. The surprised bully accepted the gift with a confused grin. All week Fran had made an extreme effort to befriend Maryjo. Due to her efforts, the daily intimidation sessions miraculously subsided. It had been the first time during the school year that Fran wasn't afraid to go to school.

This week, Fran had second thoughts about the ethics of handing over her completed homework to Maryjo. She worked so hard to get a good grade, and Maryjo did nothing at all. It just didn't seem fair. She didn't give her homework to Maryjo for one day, and this was her payment, a nasty drubbing in the bushes.

BACKGROUND INFORMATION

Fran's mother, Wella, has suspected for some time that something is wrong. It seems that almost every morning Fran complains about a different minor illness—nausea, headaches, lightheadedness. When Wella confronts Fran about her illnesses, Fran cries and says that she wants to stay home from school because she doesn't feel very good.

"If I just stay home today, I'll feel better," Fran insists in a tearful, babyish tone.

If Wella probes further, Fran's crying increases until she begins coughing and choking with tears. If Wella suggests that she call the school, Fran becomes very defensive, insisting that nothing is wrong in school. She just feels sick. Without Fran's knowledge, on one occasion Wella has called the school and spoken to her teacher, Nora Johanson. Mrs. Johanson told Wella that she had not noticed anything different in Fran's behavior, although she did admit that with 30 kids, it was difficult to keep an eye on each of them.

Maryjo carefully selected her victims and chose only those who would submit to her torment and at the same time remain quiet. With Fran, she found the perfect target. Fran was one of the smartest and one of the shyest students in the class. She would easily submit to her wishes, partly because Fran feared Maryjo and her gang and partly because Fran wanted to be friends with any student in the class. New to the area, Fran badly wanted friends. At her old school, Fran had some friends, but only one or two of them could be considered true friends. For Fran her newest friendship (or manipulative partnership) was a little like having a pal in the Mafia in that such friendships come with a price tag attached.

Maryjo and her partners rule with fear. Now in the sixth grade, Maryjo can finally effectively rule the playground and other low structure school settings without older children challenging her authority. Maryjo has sought after the control and the power that comes with her strength, size (i.e., she was the tallest sixth-grade student in her class), and fierce demeanor.

In Maryjo's family, physical and verbal abuse are everyday experiences. Her stepfather, Jack Hanley, is the source of most of the abuse in their household. Through Jack's beatings, Maryjo quickly learned that hitting and intimidation are two effective and frightening methods for a powerful person to use to get what he or she wants. Mary Hanley, Maryjo's mother, puts up with the abuse because she is too afraid of her husband to take any meaningful action. Also, she is too embarrassed to admit the abuse and seek help from family, friends, or professionals. Mary often rationalizes Jack's violent actions as warranted because she did something wrong or because Maryjo was bugging her father. Jack doesn't need to be drunk to hit Mary or Maryjo, but the frequency of the beatings increases when he is intoxicated. When Jack isn't at work at the local glass factory, he can usually be found at the VFW bar. On a number of occasions, Jack and Mary have received complaints from neighbors about Maryjo's bullying behavior, but they dismiss it as typical childhood behavior.

Mrs. Johanson has had a difficult time monitoring the behavior of her 30 students. It took her 2 full months until she was able to learn all of their names. Now in her third year, Mrs. Johanson has the reputation of being a "spacey" teacher. Often underprepared and wishy-washy when handling on-the-spot decisions, she has become the butt of jokes among the school's faculty.

Mrs. Johanson has spent so much time this year dealing with behavioral problems that she has fallen drastically behind in the curriculum—compared with the other sixth-grade classes. In order to make up some of her lost time, she has sent home larger amounts of homework than she normally would, resulting in a number of parent complaints. Her current method of dealing with behavior problems is to send the culprit into the hall for 5 minutes. Once in the hallway, Mrs. Johanson usually scolds the offender and threatens to call his or her parents. If the misbehavior is very serious, she sends the child to the principal's office. Her classroom is noisy and chaotic, often a stressful place to be. When the principal observes Mrs. Johanson for her quarterly evaluation, he is overwhelmed by the beehive of motion and sound. He leaves the room with a headache and a list of critical comments on the evaluation form. With her job on the line, Mrs. Johanson has already considered looking for other jobs.

CASE 15

GAMEY SCIENCE

THE INCIDENT

"Books open. Notebooks out. Eyes on me!" bellows Mr. Entenmann. As he calls his eighth-grade science class to order, this veteran teacher attempts to hide his anxieties beneath the fullness of his strong voice. He knows that his last period class has become increasingly unsettled and unruly in the past few weeks. Officially speaking, they have not been breaking classroom or school rules; the disruptive behavior has been playful, sarcastic, subtle, and smart. The students have attempted to lure or coax Mr. Entenmann into a jousting match, a tense verbal game in which the victor controls the classroom. The result is that Mr. Entenmann has often looked silly and the day's lecture has been sidetracked, delayed, and even lost. As Mr. Entenmann calls the class to order, he is mentally prepared to ward off any such silliness.

Before Mr. Entenmann can begin his lecture, Billy calls out from the front row. "Mr. Entenmann, I've been thinking a lot about these bases and acids and I have an important question."

"Yes," replies Mr. Entenmann hesitantly, wondering whether to encourage student interest or stop the tomfoolery before it gets started.

Billy continues. "So I'm thinking about these acids and bases flowing all over the world and I want to know——" Billy pauses here, leans back in his chair with a slight grin, and looks around to see that most of the students are watching and listening. "I want to know why the whole world isn't just rotting and deteriorating and getting eaten up by all these acids. Would you please explain that?"

Mr. Entenmann bristles slightly, his neck stiffening. He doesn't want to answer because he doubts the seriousness of the question, but he knows, too, that Billy is a top student with a good reputation. "Billy, we covered that last week. Do you have your notes from the two lectures when we covered the properties of acids?"

"Sure. I take good notes," replies Billy.

As he digs into his backpack and pulls out his notebook, Hector calls out from the back of the class. "Mr. Entenmann, I don't have that in my notes," he says as he props his chair back on two legs and smiles.

"Me either," chips in Hector's buddy Felix. His voice then trails off. He lowers his head and mumbles jokingly, so that only the back half of the class can hear, "My notes don't say anything about taking acid." The back two rows of students laugh.

"Okay. Okay. Quiet down," Mr. Entenmann demands. "I'm not covering that material again. If you don't get it the first time, you'll have to borrow the notes from someone else. Or read it in the text. The section on bases and acids begins on page 147."

"Mr. Entenmann?" queries Billy softly from the front row.

"What, Billy? We need to get started on today's material."

"I found the text's coverage of bases and acids to be somewhat spotty. Can you recommend an outside source for those of us who want to read further on the topic?" Billy smiles quasi-earnestly and turns to his friend Tony for support. Tony wrinkles his brow, nods repeatedly, and looks up at the teacher with a face of exaggerated interest.

"Quiet! No more questions!" Mr. Entenmann shouts. He has lost his patience. The tone of Billy's question sounds sincere, but it seems to be sarcastic and mocking at the same time. A hand flies up in the back of the room. It is Felix. "Felix, put your hand down," snaps Mr. Entenmann. "Keep your mouths shut, take out your notebooks, and listen. It's my turn to talk." Felix groans and drops his hand.

"But teacher," Hector spouts up, shooting a glance over to Billy, "I'm concerned that the text's coverage of this content is somewhat spotty." The class erupts in laughter.

Background Information

In recent days, Mr. Entenmann has felt like he has been forced to engage in a daily wrestling match with this class. He has had particular difficulty with two pairs of boys, one seated in the front and one seated in the back. The two pairs are a sharp contrast in style, reputation, and academic standing. While he has struggled with these particular two pairs, Mr. Entenmann must admit that most of the class has joined in the games as supportive participants.

Tony and Billy sit in the front of the class. These boys are members of an informal group called the Oxs, in the hallway lingo of Spring Hill Middle School. The Oxs wear button-down, oxford cloth shirts with a polo player insignia on the breast. They are neat, polite, and well spoken. They come to class fully prepared. They demonstrate a strong interest in the subject matter. Mr. Entenmann views Tony and Billy as obviously able and talented students. He taught Billy's older sister Kendra, who went on to be valedictorian of her high school class and is now attending West Point. The boys' grades on tests and quizzes place them at the top of the class. Despite their participation in the antics detailed above, Mr. Entenmann tends to see them as basically good kids.

The back row pair are another story. Mr. Entenmann is convinced that Felix and Hector could be average students if they only tried. He is frustrated because they don't apply themselves in his class. Both boys are first-generation Mexican immigrants to this country. They wear their dark hair down to their shoulders and often let it fall over their faces, as if they are hiding from their teacher and his lecture. When Felix rolls up the sleeves of his T-shirt, he sports a blue and red American eagle tattoo on his biceps. When Mr. Entenmann sees the tattoo, he thinks to himself that an eighth-grade boy shouldn't have a tattoo. He thinks to himself that if he were that boy's father, he'd clean him up and set him on the right track.

Mr. Entenmann teaches at Spring Hill Middle School, a large public school located on the Near North Side, one of the oldest suburbs of a medium-sized city. Historically, the Near North Side was developed by German immigrants who worked at the brick works or in the building trades at the turn of the century. As the city itself changes, the population of the school district now includes students of many ethnic groups spanning across the social class spectrum. A recent influx of Mexican and Vietnamese families to the affordable neighborhoods of Near North has changed the composition of the once homogeneous Near North schools.

Mr. Entenmann has found himself baffled by the styles of talk, clothing, and behavior of the new students. He tends to think that his job was easier before the cultural composition of the school changed. Other changes have complicated matters considerably. The district administration, once a sleeping giant in the background, has recently become very progressive and vocal, arranging workshops on multicultural education and constructivist teaching approaches for all schools. Supporting this move has been the batch of new teachers who received a similarly progressive education at the university. Additionally, the Parent Teacher Association at Spring Hill Middle School has switched from holding bake sales to fund band trips to speaking out firmly in support of a multicultural curricular format.

If one were to interview Mr. Entenmann privately about these changes, one would discover that he is not so much against these developments as he is uncomfortable about them. He would say that things are changing much too fast. His students tell him that the other teachers don't lecture anymore, that he is old-fashioned. He is afraid that the district administration is "throwing the baby out with the bath water," forcing good teachers to change their tried and true teaching methods without recognizing the years of effective instruction these teachers have contributed.

Within his classroom, Mr. Entenmann feels awkward and uncertain. He has been encouraged by his building principal to send fewer students to the office on disciplinary matters. The principal wants to decrease the number of school suspensions by having the teachers and students work out more of their difficulties in the classroom. Mr. Entenmann feels somewhat inadequate in this task. He looks back fondly on the days when he could simply put his foot down and send a misbehaving student to the office.

CASE 16

HAT TRICK

THE INCIDENT

"Has anyone seen my hat?" asks Jack as he enters Tina Young's ninth-grade special education English class.

Kevin answers, "It's in your desk, you dweeb."

Jack looks in his desk, but it's not there. Maurice and Kevin break out in laughter. Mrs. Young looks up at the boys laughing in the back of the class, shakes her head, and goes back to marking off students on her roll.

Jack repeats his request, "Has anyone seen my hat?"

Kevin answers, "It's on the shelf."

Jack walks over to the shelf by the window and hops up on his toes to take a look. Nothing there. Maurice snickers.

"Kevin, stop teasing him," says Mrs. Young.

"I'm not doing anything," Kevin says with a scowl. "I thought it was there."

Jack sits down, and Maurice stops snickering.

Kevin whispers, "Check the hall. I think I saw it under a locker by the water fountain."

Jack walks out into the hall. The entire class laughs. Jack reenters the room with empty hands. Mrs. Young directs Jack back to his desk by pointing at it with an index finger.

Kevin whispers to Jack, "Check the computer station." Jack casts a doubtful eye at Kevin, then he walks to the side of the room and looks in the area of the computer station, but his hat is not there. Kevin and Maurice snicker.

"Stop it, Kevin," Mrs. Young says in her serious tone of voice.

"I thought I saw him wear it at the computer station," responds Kevin innocently.

Kevin and Maurice stop laughing, and Jack sits down. Kevin then points to under the teacher's desk. The hat was there the entire time. As Jack gets up to retrieve the hat, the entire class laughs.

BACKGROUND INFORMATION

Kevin has been Jack's nemesis since junior high school, teasing or taunting him virtually nonstop since the beginning of the new school year. Mrs. Young, their teacher, has complained to other teachers about this problem. Her colleagues agree that it is a serious problem, but no one knows how to deal with it, even though they are experienced special education teachers. Kevin is the son of Dr. Bobby Taplen, the district superintendent. Not surprisingly, Kevin has often received special treatment by teachers who were worried about saying anything negative about Dr. Taplen's boy. Kevin has gotten into trouble at school on a number of occasions, often for intimidating a peer or for fighting. Even when teachers have dared to take official disciplinary action against Kevin for his misbehavior, the standard punishments have not been administered. Typically, the principal will make a discrete phone call to Kevin's mother. She'll come pick him up, and then his parents deal with the issue privately at home. For Kevin, this usually means a pretty mild reprimand from either his mother or father. Kevin is well aware of his father's influence in school. He has told his fellow classmates, "Teachers can't touch me because my dad's the boss."

Kevin is the only child in the Taplen family. Darlene and Bobby work very hard, both usually work overtime, in order to provide a comfortable life for Kevin. As a result of their work schedules, Kevin frequently goes unsupervised in the afternoon or early evening hours. When Kevin is at home, he spends most of his time in his room watching TV, exploring the Internet, or listening to rock music. When not at home, Kevin can usually be found at Maurice's house. Kevin and Maurice often talk about their evening escapades, replaying old classics and planning new mischievous adventures that typically involve acts of petty theft and vandalism upon their neighbors, from covering old man Simpson's weeping willow tree with toilet paper to feeding Valium to Mrs. Bleecher's poodle. (The dog died. Nobody figured out who did it. Kevin and Maurice both felt guilty but rationalized their crime by telling themselves that it was an accident. They only meant to put the dog to sleep for a few hours.)

To deal with Kevin's problems, he is receiving counseling from Dr. Henry Wallen, an adolescent psychologist. During his counseling sessions, Kevin has admitted that many of his behaviors can be controlled. But he often doesn't feel like doing the right thing or living by the rules. Kevin can't stand to live the drab life his parents live; he says it's too boring. He wants excitement, and the best kind of excitement is transgressing on forbidden territory. Through therapy, he has also admitted that he doesn't feel that his parents care about him. They are busy with their careers. Also, Kevin feels that he and his parents are utterly dissimilar. They walk the straight and narrow while he wants to walk on the wildest edge of the wild side. He thinks that he must have been adopted.

Dr. Wallen has discussed his concerns about Kevin with Kevin's parents. Darlene is a strong believer that the therapy is helping Kevin; however, Bobby doesn't like the therapist and consequently does not always follow up on Dr. Wallen's recommendations. Instead, Bobby feels that "grounding" Kevin is the best solution for most of Bobby's inappropriate behavior. In one recent incident, Bobby caught Kevin beating up a younger teenager. When he asked Kevin why he did it, Kevin replied, "He needs to learn a lesson that nobody backtalks Kevin Taplen." Bobby told him that he used poor judgment and grounded him for the weekend. Kevin's sentence was especially painful because that night was the school's big football game against Ross High School. As Kevin ran to his room he yelled out, "All you care about is being a big shot!" When he slammed the door behind him, Bobby followed. Bobby approached the door, but he stopped and did not enter. He didn't know what to say, didn't know how to make things better. Kevin did not speak to his father that entire weekend. Even today, the two rarely speak.

Kevin's teasing of Jack is not an isolated incident. Kevin is a large, strong boy who frequently bullies other students. Kevin has been known to humiliate other students to the point that they cry.

Mrs. Young is quick to point out that Kevin is proud of himself after his bullying sessions with other children. She, a firm believer in behavioral approaches to managing behaviors, feels that Kevin should not be reinforced by teachers for his inappropriate behavior. She believes that students want only one type of reinforcement in school, and that is teacher attention. Because of her belief, she tries to use planned ignoring for any inappropriate behavior and uses teacher reinforcement for all appropriate behavior. In Kevin's case, she is simply befuddled that she can't extinguish his teasing behavior.

CASE **17**

Repeating History or History Repeating Itself

The Incident

"In 1775, what famous American warned other villagers in Lexington, Massachusetts, that the British were coming?" Jane Rutherman asked her ninth-grade history class. As she scanned the room for raised hands, she noticed that Felicia, once again, had her head down on her desk and appeared to be sleeping. "Jill what is the answer?" Mrs. Rutherman queried.

"Paul Revere?" Jill answered with some hesitation in her voice.

"That's right!" Mrs. Rutherman replied. Jane was proud of the students in her class because she felt that they already had learned so much history since the start of school only 3 weeks ago—with the exception of Felicia, that is. "Felicia, please sit up!" Mrs. Rutherman said in a quiet voice so as not to call attention to the student. Mrs. Rutherman knew that she somehow lost young Felicia in her quest to teach history to the entire class, but she also did not see how she could individualize her instruction for just one student.

Writing notes on the board as she lectured, Mrs. Rutherman noticed that while Felicia had managed to stay awake, she did not copy very many notes down in her notebook. When Mrs. Rutherman walked around the room to monitor students' notetaking, she saw Felicia's pages covered with the names of famous rock bands and the words *History died. Let's move on.* As Mrs. Rutherman finished her lecture the bell rang, but before students could leave, she reminded them about the Monday quiz. Almost all of the students made a note of this on their papers, except Felicia who closed her book and walked out of class. After Felicia left class, Mrs. Rutherman asked herself, "What can I do to get this student involved?"

Background Information

Jane was starting her second year of teaching. After a successful first year, she was poised and confident as she taught. Although much of the class time was spent lecturing, her enthusiasm for history had helped to keep the discussions and lectures lively. Students asked questions about information that they did not understand, and Jane provided imaginative stories about actual events. The give-and-take of this style of presenting information had made Jane one of the best first-year history teachers in the district. Despite her pride in her teaching and her contagious enthusiasm, at the end of the day she would become upset about the one or two students whom she could not reach. Felicia was one of them. Only 3 weeks into the semester, Felicia had earned a C and a D on the two announced quizzes.

Jane, concerned about Felicia, began to ask herself a series of questions: "Was Felicia lazy?" "Does Felicia have a learning or reading problem?" "Can Felicia take notes?" "Does Felicia study for the quizzes?" The next day Jane decided to look over Felicia's school records. To her amazement, Felicia's IQ was listed as 127, and her grades had been average to above average over the past 3 years. She then checked with Felicia's other teachers to find that she had started the school year off very poorly in most of her subjects, a dramatic change from her prior performance. Armed with this information, she decided to schedule an after-class meeting with Felicia.

That next day when class had finished, Jane asked Felicia to stay after so that she could talk to her. Felicia agreed, and the two sat down at a large table in the back to talk.

"Look Felicia, I know that you are an intelligent girl. I can't understand why you don't pay attention in my class. Your records show that you are a good student," Mrs. Rutherman said.

Felicia was slow to respond, but eventually spoke up and said, "History is a real drag, and your voice just puts me to sleep."

Mrs. Rutherman, trying to hold back her amazement at Ruth's candid response, followed up with another question, "Well, what don't you like about history or the way I teach it?" Felicia, feeling uncomfortable, replied, "Let's just face it. I don't like you and you don't like me. End of story."

Mrs. Rutherman wanting to avoid a confrontation, tried to change the subject by asking about Felicia's home, "Is there something going on at home that I should know about?"

To that question, Felicia quickly responded, "Its none of your damn business! I'm outa here!" Felicia then took off for the door.

As she walked out, Mrs. Rutherman yelled out, "If you fail history, you'll have to repeat it this summer." Then Mrs. Rutherman murmured under her breath, "History repeating itself." With the irony of that statement, Jane sat in her chair and shook her head. Reflecting on their conversation, she wasn't certain how well she had done or what step to take next. Jane had thought of calling Felicia's mother, Rosie, but her experiences with Lucia, Felicia's older sister, had prevented the phone call. Jane had had similar problems with Lucia and had tried to contact her mother, but after three attempts, she had been unable to contact her. She then tried to mail a letter to her house, but it was returned as undeliverable. So she gave up on Lucia, who ended up passing with a C-. Perhaps there was still hope for Felicia.

Once at home, Felicia complains to Lucia that the "history Nazi" is giving her a hassle. Felicia's sister, a senior in high school, dislikes most of her teachers and is wary of adult authority figures. She too has confrontations with her teachers, and so she empathizes with Felicia's problems. As her role model, Lucia has taught Felicia how to smoke marijuana and drink hard liquor. For Felicia, these "escapes" are just the thing to do on weekends. Felicia, although a good student, can't see the connection between history (as well as other school subjects) and her vocational goal of working at the Farside Music store. Felicia's love for rock music has helped her to set this rather humble goal.

After school, Felicia often turns up the speakers and listens to music with her sister, before their parents arrive home. At her sister's prodding, Felicia has smoked marijuana on a number of occasions. As she smokes, she imagines herself partying with Benji "Gimme" Moore, the lead drummer of Dead Cat Skins. As she likes to say, "Life is a party. Drink while you can and to hell with school, to hell with the world" (the lyrics from the Blown Away album by the Dead Cat Skins).

CASE **18**

HOMEWORK TIME

THE INCIDENT

Gretchen Schmitz plopped down on the couch and closed her eyes. It had been a long day at the office, and the evening battle over homework was yet to begin. Within seconds, the briefcase had slipped from Gretchen's hands to the floor as she drifted into sleep. Her husband Charley was away on business all week. Her 10-year-old son, also Charley, was upstairs in his bedroom playing video games and hoping his mother wouldn't call out those dreaded words: *Homework time!*

When Gretchen awoke, it was almost 8 o'clock, long past the official 7 o'clock start of homework time for little Charley. Gretchen walked up the stairs to find Charley still playing video games. She sighed. She hadn't really expected to see him propped up at his desk with his pencil grinding away on tonight's math problems. For once, though, it would be nice if he would take responsibility for his own homework.

"Let's go, champ," Gretchen said as she motioned Charley to his desk and pulled up a second chair for herself. She sat down.

Charley left the video game running and jumped onto his bed. Rolling up in his covers, he groaned, "Oh, Mom, not again."

"Yes, again," Gretchen said as she felt her internal thermometer rising. She had little patience for this nightly tussle. "And again and again and again. How do you think your father and I got to where we are today? We did our homework every night for 12 years, then 4 more, then even more after that."

Charley wrapped the pillow around his head and ignored his mother's words. He repeated softly, "And law school is the most difficult of all, most difficult of all, most difficult of all."

Gretchen took three deep breaths. She felt the growing tension in her forehead and reminded herself that she had had a long day at work. She could envision herself about to snap, about to start shouting and grabbing little Charley by the arm. She closed her eyes and took two more deep breaths and imagined herself sitting on the Adirondack chair on the back porch of their weekend cottage. The breeze through the pines was soft and fragrant. Finally, she opened her eyes and said, "Okay, Charley, we up the ante."

"Up?" Charley's face popped up from behind the pillow. "How much?"

"We'll double it. That's 20 cents a problem for math and 30 cents per comprehension question in reading. But that's only for correct answers."

"I know," Charley said as he leaped out of bed and rushed over to his desk. He imitated his father's deep voice, "Nobody pays anyone to do a job poorly." With that, Charley quickly opened his reading text and began to read the assigned story in his reading book.

BACKGROUND INFORMATION

The Schmitz household runs on a very tight schedule. Gretchen and Charley are both successful lawyers for a major firm. They drive each morning from their large suburban home into the downtown business district. Generally only one of the two parents is able to come home in time to pick up little Charley at the sitter's house and supervise his homework. Since both parents have more than ample work responsibilities, they often squabble over who can work late and who must go home to pick up their son. Gretchen often finds herself fulfilling the child care role, thereby sacrificing some of her career aspirations and allowing her husband a greater chance to excel at the firm. She has mixed emotions about doing this. She feels her heart pull her toward her son while she also silently resents the assumed gender roles played out in the arrangement. Due to his parents' demanding schedules, little Charley almost always eats dinner at the sitter's house.

The Schmitzes were both excellent students throughout their many years of education. They have difficulty comprehending their son's reluctance to do academic work and his evident struggles to do well.

Little Charley is a fourth grader at the Clifton School, a small and expensive private school. His teachers have consistently expressed concern that Charley's reading skills have been developing slowly. Recent testing places his reading comprehension and decoding skills in the second-grade range, a markedly low score for a student at Clifton. His mathematics scores are average for his age, and his general informational knowledge is well above average.

At the most recent parent-teacher conference, Ms. Curwin, Charley's teacher, hesitantly voiced the possibility of a learning disability to Charley's mother. The professionals at Clifton often feel pressure to deliver high achievement from students, since the students' parents are generally highly educated and financially successful. Suggesting that a parent seek testing for a learning disability is very difficult for the teachers to do. Additionally, knowing that they work in a school with an extremely low teacher-student ratio and the best curricular materials and educational technology available, the teachers take enormous personal responsibility for their students' learning. They are very slow to suggest that a child may have a learning disability.

The words *learning disability* flew right past Mrs. Schmitz as she quickly stated that Charley would simply work harder. She and her husband tend to downplay the extent of Charley's academic weaknesses, assuming instead that he is a late bloomer who will soon "grow out of it."

The evening struggle over homework has blossomed into a tremendous nightly headache for both mother and son. Two weeks before the incident detailed above, Gretchen called Ms. Curwin to seek her advice. How could she get Charley to do his homework without a nightly battle? Ms. Curwin suggested using a behavior modification program through which Charley would earn small rewards for completing his homework.

Gretchen pulled out her old psychology textbook from college and read the section on behavior modification. She set up a reinforcement system whereby Charley would receive 1 point for each school assignment completed. Upon reaching 25 points, he would have earned the new video game, Night of the Frog Ranger, that he had been begging for recently. Unfortunately, this plan held Charley's interest for only five evenings. On the sixth evening, Charley counted his points and moaned, "This deal isn't fair. It'll take me to forever to get the Frog Ranger." This complaint sparked an argument between the mother and son about the fairness of the reward system.

Gretchen is frustrated. They used to argue over the homework itself. Now they have "progressed" to arguing about the reinforcers. She has observed that Charley seems more interested in sustaining the conflict with his parents than in earning the game. Additionally, she wonders if earning rewards is all that appealing anyway. She has had to admit that her son already owns so many toys that his room can hardly contain them. Why would the kid who has everything want to earn more stuff?

Exasperated, Gretchen turned to her husband, who declared, "Forget the points. No one wants to earn points. Pay him cash. I work for money. You work for money. Let him work for money." The next day Gretchen started paying little Charley for completing his homework. The effectiveness of financial rewards has been inconsistent. Some evenings little Charley is excited about earning the cash. Other nights he seems to care less about earning rewards.

Gretchen has decided to set up a meeting with Ms. Curwin to seek additional advice. Perhaps they are doing the reinforcement program in the wrong way. The way the psychology textbook explains behavior modification makes it seem highly precise and technical. Maybe they are doing it wrong. Gretchen also wonders whether a different approach to changing Charley's behavior might be more effective.

CASE 19

HOPE

THE INCIDENT

Twenty-two second-grade students are seated around tables in small groups. Mrs. Caulfield is talking the groups through a rather complicated series of directions for the next activity. Repeatedly the students turn away from their teacher to watch Hope, the tall girl at the back of the room who is playing a computer game. She is shouting loudly and swinging her long arms in the air. A special classroom aide assigned to work individually with Hope tries to calm and focus her, encouraging her to play quietly and place her free hand on her lap. Hope is seated with her back to her classmates. She spins around in her seat and sizes up the many eyes that are focusing on her. Her individual aide, Mrs. Tedesky, sets a gentle hand on her shoulder and tries to reposition the student to face the computer screen. Hope wriggles to get free. Her arms swing vigorously through the air, and she whines loudly, drawing the attention of her classmates away from their school tasks. As Mrs. Tedesky tries to grab her waving arms, Hope slides down in her chair, slipping away from her aide's grasp and dropping down to the floor. She then crawls beneath the table to the back wall, far from Mrs. Tedesky's reach.

By now Mrs. Caulfield has lost the attention of the rest of the class. She tells the groups to review the directions she has given them thus far and then rushes over to help Mrs. Tedesky.

Mrs. Tedesky is down on her knees, peering under the table at Hope. "Come out of there right now or you won't get any recess," the aide insists. Hope doesn't budge. She pulls her knees into her stomach and begins to rock back and forth. Mrs. Caulfield kneels down, looks under the table, and wonders what to do.

BACKGROUND INFORMATION

When Irene Danesi decided to go back to school for her master's degree, she packed up her home and her 8-year-old daughter Hope and moved a hundred miles to an apartment near the university. She called the local school district to arrange a meeting to discuss an appropriate class placement for Hope. The previous school district diagnosed Hope as having a mild form of autism, a condition typically characterized by social withdrawal, poor social skills, limited cognitive and/or language ability, and patterns of ritualistic, repetitive behavior. For example, one common characteristic is echolalia, a speech pattern in which the individual repeats back the final word or words of the phrase spoken to her. Hope rarely does this. She is considered a "high-functioning autistic." She is considered to have the general cognitive and language skills of a 5-year-old, which allows her to carry on conversations and work on early math and reading skills.

Although Hope's previous school district had placed her in a self-contained program for students diagnosed with autism, Irene hoped that the new school would arrange for her daughter to be mainstreamed into a third-grade general education class. Irene was concerned that Hope's oral language skills were receiving inadequate attention in the self-contained class where few of her peers had the ability to carry on a conversation. She thought that a general education classroom would provide a richer context for language development.

The new school district agreed to place Hope in a general classroom but insisted on a second-grade instead of a third-grade setting. They reasoned that Hope might do better both socially and academically among younger students. They assigned Hope to Mrs. Caulfield's class because Mrs. Caulfield had worked successfully the year before with a boy with Down's syndrome. Mrs. Caulfield agreed reluctantly, saying that she knew next to nothing about autism but that she was willing to learn. A one-to-one teacher aide, Mrs. Tedesky, was assigned to help Hope complete her academic lessons. While the other students sit in the traditional rows, Mrs. Caulfield gave Hope her own special seat at the back of the class, where she and Mrs. Tedesky could work in isolation.

After 2 weeks of Hope's loud behavior, Mrs. Caulfield called Hope's mother to discuss the situation. She described Hope's behavior and explained her three concerns. First, according to school records, Hope's agitated and anxious classroom behavior in these initial 2 weeks diverges sharply from her school behavior in prior years. The special education teacher who taught Hope during the previous year described her as a generally calm and pleasant child. Mrs. Caulfield is wondering why the switch to the general second-grade classroom has brought on such a flurry of energy and motion. Or maybe the special education teacher was sugar-coating the story, making Hope appear behaviorally better than she really was. Second, Hope's odd behavior has already attracted the scorn of her peers. The children are avoiding working and playing with Hope. Mrs. Caulfield is concerned about the kind of friendships Hope will be able to develop with peers who already avoid her. Finally, in terms of specific behaviors, Mrs.

Caulfield notes that Hope's extremely loud tone of voice is the most disruptive aspect of her current presentation.

Mrs. Caulfield could tell that Irene was anxious, barely holding back tears as they talked about the difficulties Hope was experiencing. "You'll have to excuse my ignorance, Mrs. Danesi, but is speaking very loudly a part of Hope's autism?"

"No, not really, not so far," Irene replied. "Is she too loud in class?"

"Yes, she shouts out pretty much throughout the day. It distracts the other students."

"She's never been loud like that. What is she shouting?"

"I don't know. All sort of things—when she gets frustrated or when she wants something."

"You're not going to pull her from the mainstream, are you?" Irene asked in an almost desperate tone.

"No, its much too early for such a drastic step," Mrs. Caulfield assured the mother. "It may be simply a transitional problem that smooths itself out as Hope becomes more accustomed to the new classroom. Has she ever been in a regular classroom?"

"No. She's been in the special programs all along. Does that make a difference?"

"It might. The special classes are very different from my class. They have very few students. They're often highly structured," commented the teacher. "Hope seems bewildered by her new situation. I'm wondering if the big room and the large number of students are frightening to her. Has she told you anything?"

"She's been really stirred up at home. This morning I had quite a bit of trouble even getting her onto the bus. She's usually not like that. She's always liked going to school."

Mrs. Caulfield paused to think. Then she asked, "Has Hope said anything specific about what she doesn't like?"

"All I know is she doesn't like some kid named T."

"T?"

"Yeah. I found a page in her coloring book with the letter *T* written over and over and crossed out every time. Who is T?"

"Mrs. Tedesky, her aide. The kids call her 'Mizz' T."

"Why doesn't she like her aide?" Irene asked.

"I don't know. She seems nice enough to me. The other students like her. There must be something going on here that I haven't noticed."

"Now that I know who T is, I can ask Hope some questions. And maybe you can talk to the aide about this. I'm surprised she's starting hating "Mizz" T so quickly. There have been a few teachers she wasn't crazy about in the past, but it never happened so fast.

"Well, what sort of teachers didn't she like in the past?" queried Mrs. Caulfield.

"Hmmm, well, in the first grade, she didn't like her bus driver. Miss Grace, I think. Hope was afraid of her. Miss Grace usually had a nice way with the children. But when she got mad, she could be mean and intimidating. She would punish Hope for the littlest thing. Then there was the speech therapist at her old school, Mr. Antaki, an enormous man with a booming voice. Now that I think of it, she was afraid of him, too. I guess it was his big voice. In fact, he used to sing quite a bit. She hated that. I don't know why, but she hated it."

"It sounds like we need to look into this further to find out what is going on between Hope and Mrs. Tedesky. Why don't we both check on our own end and talk again tomorrow night?"

"Okay," agreed Hope's mother. "We'll get to the bottom of this."

CASE 20

IMAGE MANAGEMENT

THE INCIDENT

"Tyler, this is the third time they've sent you to see me this month," Mr. Secaucus wheezed, in a foghorn voice, through the midnight darkness of his office. He fingered the edges of a manila file and occasionally peered at the paper contents. Tyler, the accused 10th grader, sat across from the guidance counselor's desk. His black leather biker's jacket squeaked as he shifted nervously about in the tiny chair provided for him. Occasionally his left hand toyed with a small gold ring that looped through the side of his nose. The blinds were drawn tightly to hold out the sunlight. Only a small desk lamp located midway between the counselor and student cast light upon the situation.

"Um, four."

"What?"

"I think this is the fourth time," Tyler corrected the veteran counselor.

"Really?" The counselor leaned his large, round face into the light and pulled his reading glasses down to the tip of his nose. "You say four?"

"Well, there were three times for skipping detention. I mean, I skipped twice for each time. Six total skips, but you don't get sent to the Big Tuna, I mean, to see you, uh, unless you skip twice."

"And what did you get those three detentions for in the first place? I don't recall." Mr. Secaucus settled his large body back in his chair and laughed to himself. He hadn't heard that "Big Tuna" nickname since the early eighties.

"Smoking in the boys' room. Coach Wilkes likes to catch me between second and third period." Tyler smiled hesitantly. He seemed to be gaining a little confidence as the session progressed.

"Coach likes to catch you, and you like to get caught?"

"I need the cigarette, you know. And it seems to make his day to catch me. Like if he can't win enough football games, at least he's nailing me to the wall."

Mr. Secaucus chuckled. "I'm glad to hear you feel some indebtedness to our beleaguered football coach. I guess someone *should* bolster his self-esteem a bit after last year's loss to Lakeville."

"And Southside, Phillipsburg, East Ridge——"

"Okay Tyler, I get the point. Coach Wilkes can definitely use a little pick-me-up to help his damaged spirits. I'm just wondering why it has to be you."

"Just trying to do my community service, I guess."

"Uh-huh. I see." The counselor paused for a second to consider the situation. He was well aware that Tyler's older brother Kelly was the star halfback for the football team. Kelly was well known in this small town high school as the proverbial big man on campus—a star athlete, favorite of the girls, and National Honor Society student. In contrast, Tyler seemed like a confused thug wanna-be with a new nose ring and a cheap leather jacket. One could never tell whether Tyler was actually heading down the wrong path or simply trifling with trouble in order to cultivate a tough-guy image. "Well," Mr. Secaucus continued, "what it this fourth offense that brings you to me today?"

"Mrs. West caught me trying to leave the school grounds."

"You were skipping her class again?"

"Hey, how'd you know. I mean, yeah, not *again* really. Not like I'm not there all the time. I'm almost always in Mrs. West's class."

Mr. Secaucus peered through his reading glasses at the folder in his hands. It was too dark to read. He then leaned forward under the desk lamp to read the file. "It says here that you've missed Mrs. West's third period class 15 times in the past 4 months. Your grades have dropped markedly in English and history. What's the deal? I thought she was your favorite. She helps you keep up in your other classes. Without her, you'd be sunk."

Tyler shrugged his shoulders with an odd grin. "I guess so. I'm sinking all right."

"Tyler, you've got to be sinking for Mrs. West to write you up. She's the last one to write up a disciplinary action on a student. She must be worried to death about you."

The accused and the counselor sat for a minute in the darkness. Tyler alternately smiled as if he were pulling a fast one and frowned the worrisome frown of a small boy who is about to disappoint his parents again. Mr. Secaucus rummaged through his files for Tyler's home phone number. He punched the digits on the phone and wondered silently why this boy was making such an extreme but only partially successful effort to seem nonchalant in the midst of obvious failure.

BACKGROUND INFORMATION

It would be an understatement to say that the 308 students of Polk High School know each other. They know each other in that intimate, rumor-filled, supportive yet style-cramping way that only happens in a small mountain town. On Friday nights, you can be sure to find every citizen at the high school football game, cheering on the Polk Panthers, grumbling about bad officiating, and catching up on the news of the past week. On Sunday morning, the bleach-pale coal miners, dressed in snug suits wearing thin at the elbows, humbly line the church pews with their wives and children. Then they go off to the pancake house or Morrison's Cafeteria for a brunch that could satisfy Goliath.

Clyde and Delores Eldredge have two sons, Tyler and Kelly. Clyde is well liked around town. He owns and operates the Krispy Kreme donut store on the corner of Main and Jefferson. He is past president of the school board and current leader of the Polk Chamber of Commerce. He is considered the "salt of the earth," a regular kind of guy who will happily refill your coffee while you gripe about the government or lend a pickup truck and a helping hand when you can't fit all that firewood you bought into the back of your own truck.

Few people in Polk would call Clyde an alcoholic. Friends would prefer instead to say that he likes a cold beer now and then. Truthfully, Clyde has struggled with an alcohol abuse problem for years. He tends to be a quiet, solitary sort of drunk who stays at home and drinks beer while he fiddles with half-completed projects in his garage workshop. His family and friends have helped him to conceal his problem, and he remains in the good graces of the community that praises him. In the last 6 months, since Dolores finished her associate's degree and started attending Long Notch College, Clyde's drinking has increased noticeably. Although he has not complained, Clyde has felt betrayed his wife's extensive time out of the home and her obvious success in an academic world far beyond his 10th-grade education.

When the boys were little, Dolores was a stay-at-home kind of mom. Once the boys reached high school, she found herself getting restless in the big empty house, so she started taking courses at the community college. Now she drives over an hour each way to take courses at the 4-year college on the other side of the mountain. She hopes to earn a degree in journalism and write for the town newspaper.

The sibling rivalry between 17-year-old Kelly and his 16-year-old brother Tyler has never been obvious. The boys played well together as youngsters. Once Kelly reached junior high school, the two boys seemed to go their separate ways. Kelly climbed to the top of every achievement mountain in sight. He excelled in academics and sports. In contrast, Tyler found reading and writing to be nearly impossible chores. He and his mother would sit at the kitchen table for long hours each evening, his eyes pouring over the strange shapes on the page, his mouth endlessly repeating initial consonant sounds. The two ended up in tears and arguments on many evenings.

Tyler was diagnosed with a learning disability in the fifth grade. At that time, testing indicated that his reading and writing skills were two to three grade levels behind his classmates. He received extra help in a resource room throughout his junior high school years. His literacy skills improved very slowly. He struggled in all academic areas except mathematics and music. With his parents' support and divine auditory patience, he took up the drums. They bought him a drum kit, and he practiced each night in the basement. By the time he entered Polk High School, Tyler had written off the academic world as personally unfulfilling while excelling as drummer for both the school marching band and award-winning jazz band.

At Polk High School, Tyler is taking the standard 10th-grade classes. The learning disabilities program at Polk consists of a resource class that operates like a continuously rolling study hall. Mrs. West is the teacher, a veteran of 16 years in the classroom. She likes to keep her resource room low key and relaxed. Students are typically assigned to her class for one or two periods per day. They enter, sit wherever they want, and work on assignments for their "mainstream" classes. Mrs. West views herself as an all-purpose tutor who can help students on an as-needed basis. Often students need assistance in understanding the material presented in class or in the subject area texts. Mrs. West has worked many hours to produce detailed outlines of text chapters in the various subject areas. Also, she helps students study for tests. Many of her students can grasp the conceptual and factual content of American history or biology but cannot demonstrate this knowledge on the tests.

Tyler is assigned to attend Mrs. West's class third period each day. His attendance and effort over the past year have been inconsistent. At times, he has worked closely with Mrs. West. She has taught him note taking and test preparation skills. He has benefited from a small English study group, a group of three 10th-grade boys who help each other comprehend and analyze the complex pieces of literature required for class.

CASE 21

A Blue Ink Line

The Incident

Six of the eight students in Mr. Rose's class were working quietly. Little Dougie was toying with something in his desk, probably an eraser shaped like a superhero or a race car with battery operated lights that shined clear to the back of his desk. Mr. Rose ignored him for the moment. His attention was on Celia as she struggled with her spelling assignment. She was working very hard, but not very quietly. Her face was red and tense. Every 5 seconds or so she sighed or moaned. Occasionally she struck her fist against the side of her leg. Mr. Rose rolled his teacher's chair up to the 9-year-old's desk.

"You seem a little frustrated. Can I give you some help?"

"This book is so stupid," the exasperated youngster replied. "Stooo-pid. Stooo-pid. Stoooo-pid."

"What don't you understand?" asked the teacher.

"All of it. Its so stupid. Stooo-pid!" Celia rapped her pencil nervously against the desk as she spoke.

Mr. Rose leaned in to examine her paper. She had spelled the first eight words correctly. On number nine, she had incorrectly spelled *avenue* A-V-A-N-U-E. As Mr. Rose reached his pen across to write on her paper, she gasped. She quickly pushed his hand aside. His pen had made a half-inch, blue ink line on her paper. She rubbed the line furiously with her pencil eraser, but it would not come out. Then she burst into tears.

"You ruined it! You ruined it!" she cried.

"Celia," Mr. Rose attempted to calm her, "it's okay. It's only a little line."

"No! You ruined it! Why did you do that? You ruined everything!" she shouted repeatedly, the tears rolling down her angry face. She jumped out of her seat and snatched up her chair. She held her chair over her head. Mr. Rose backed away. She stepped toward him, a tiny girl carrying a large chair. She repeatedly threatened, "I'm going to hurt you. I'm going to break your head."

BACKGROUND INFORMATION

Celia is a student at the Durham School, a public school day treatment program for students diagnosed with severe emotional and behavioral disorders. She entered the program only a week before the above incident. That first week had passed without an apparent problem, although Mr. Rose noticed that Celia seemed obsessive and perfectionistic in regard to both her appearance and the orderliness of her possessions. For example, she had a particular place in her desk for her pencil box, her notebooks, her textbooks, and her hair brush. She also did not like her peers to touch her, even if by accident.

Prior to admission to the Durham School, Celia reportedly had many behavior problems at both her previous school and at home. These problems seemed to reach a crescendo in recent weeks when Celia experienced a number of disruptive episodes in school. Her third-grade teacher, Miss Stanfield, had finally realized that she simply didn't know how to run a safe and positive learning environment with Celia in the class. On three occasions, Celia exploded into a rage, flipping her desk upside down, tossing her books about the room, and shouting obscenities at her teacher.

Throughout the year, Celia had been very stubborn, often refusing to follow her teacher's directions or mumbling under her breath in response to those directions. There were days when Celia's mood seemed fixed and negative, when she wouldn't allow anyone to tell her what to do. Miss Stanfield coped with Celia's moods by allowing her freedom to choose her activities. If the class was working on a social studies lesson and Celia refused, Miss Stanfield allowed Celia to choose another activity. Miss Stanfield was pleased if the rest of the group could go on with their work while Celia busied herself with her own choice. This tactic had been effective, due primarily to the fact that while Celia can be very obstinate, she is far from lazy. She enjoys keeping herself busy. If given a choice of activities, she quickly picks one and buries herself in the work.

In Celia's final month in the general education class, Miss Stanfield observed that Celia's tension and anger seemed heightened, as if something were making every little conflict and problem rise to a heightened sense of urgency. Negotiating the choice of activities with Celia, previously a quick and simple task, had become as difficult as management-union negotiations during a strike. Celia balked and wrangled over the choices. She complained that the choices were no good. She seemed to want to engage her teacher in an angry conflict.

Additionally, while Celia had not been a particularly close friend with her classmates, she seemed further estranged from the group. Miss Stanfield heard reports from two girls that Celia had pushed them and threatened to hurt them.

At home, Celia lives with her mother Terese, her father Will, and her 6-year-old sister Candace. Will works long hours as a line repairman for the local electric company. He generally remains silent during meetings with school personnel, allowing his wife to do the talking. Terese is a hair stylist. She is very worried about Celia's behavior. She sometimes thinks that Celia's behavior must be due to her own incompetence as a mother.

Candace has apparently not had behavior problems, though Celia's parents report that Celia and Candace often argue and fight. Candace is often the target of Celia's anger. The girls' parents admit that Candace provokes Celia, but they generally claim that Celia is the center of the problem.

Terese and Will have been married for 10 years. They report that their marriage and home life have been happy until Celia's recent instances of misbehavior. In the past 3 months, Terese has had increasing difficulty getting Celia to comply with her mother's directions. For example, one evening when Will was working late, Terese decided to take the two girls shopping at the supermarket. As they shopped, Celia refused to stay by her mother's side. She wandered around the store on her own. When the time came to load the groceries into the car and go home, Celia would not get in the car. Terese and Celia had a 20 minute standoff in the parking lot. Celia repeatedly stated that she would only get in the car if she got the front seat and her younger sister rode in the back. Since it was Candace's turn to sit in the front seat, Terese would not give in to Celia's demands. Celia's talk soon deteriorated from demanding the front seat to saying that she wouldn't ride unless they left Candace behind. Finally, after 20 minutes of embarrassment in the middle of the busy parking lot, Terese let Celia ride up front. Candace cried all the way home, and Terese felt like she was failing as a mother.

Terese and Will are hopeful about Celia's behavior and emotional state improving at the Durham School, a well-staffed, therapeutic program for troubled youngsters in Grades K through 5. The program consists of six classrooms of eight students, each staffed by a special education teacher and an aide. The support staff includes a crisis teacher who helps individual teachers handle behavior outbursts and instances of conflict in the classroom. Additionally, the school is served by two professionals with mental health training, a guidance counselor, and a social worker. Each of these professionals provide group therapy for the students, consult with teachers on issues of emotion and behavior, and work with parents on dealing with family problems. The principal of the Durham School views himself as a hands-off manager whose job is to handle the bureaucratic red tape so that his staff can do as they see fit.

While the Durham School staff holds the overall goal of preparing troubled students to re-enter the general education mainstream, they are rarely successful in doing so. Less than 10% of their students ever return to general education classrooms. The teachers and support staff blame this fact on the severity of the students' emotional/behavioral problems, the lack of effort by many parents to work closely with the school, and reluctance of general education teachers and building principals to give troubled students a second chance.

CASE 22

WHEN A JOKE IS NO LONGER A JOKE

THE INCIDENT

"When was the last time Mrs. Drudge had a man?" Betty whispers across the classroom to Joan and Eddie.

Interested but wanting to avoid trouble, the two students silently mouth, "I don't know. When?"

"The night after she got her first set of wooden teeth," Betty responds.

A handful of students laugh half-aloud. Mrs. Drudge, busy writing notes on the board, turns around and tells the class to be quiet. Betty remains quiet for a few minutes, but then cracks another joke. The students seated near her again laugh at her joke. Mrs. Drudge, trying to ignore the behavior, continues working at the board. A third time Betty makes another joke and again the class laughs. Mrs. Drudge again ignores the laughter. Within minutes, Betty makes a silly face behind Mrs. Drudge's back and again the class laughs. This time, Mrs. Drudge points to Betty and says, "Quiet down." Betty is silent for a few minutes, but then she thinks of another joke.

Betty makes a face and comments, "I need a fix. I have a Drudge problem." Her classmates again roar. When Mrs. Drudge looks for the guilty party, students' eyes point in Betty's direction. This little scenario repeats itself three times until Mrs. Drudge finally sends Betty into the hall.

BACKGROUND INFORMATION

Although it's only the second week of classes, Betty has been in trouble a number of times. Betty enjoys being the class clown, but often pays the price—her parents ground her for a day or two for each school incident. She has been the class clown for a number of years and, in the process, has managed to wreak havoc upon many of her teachers. At home, even as a child, Betty would often put on evening "shows" consisting of dancing, songs, jokes, and exaggerated imitations of famous movie stars. She entertained her mother for hours. Humor runs in the family. Her mother's witty sarcasm and her father's unequaled comedic timing have combined to produce a very funny little girl. But that very funny girl has a hidden, dark secret: She suffers from depression.

Perhaps it is through her humor that Betty has creatively struggled through her deep bouts of melancholy, hopelessness, and lethargy. Diagnosed as having a chronic, moderate form of depression since the age of 11, Betty has managed the various depressive symptoms through a combination of medication, humor, and support. Her parents, Phil and Mill Parot, have provided tremendous love and support through the years. They have taken Betty to various doctors in an attempt to find the optimal treatment for her.

Now 15, Betty currently uses a three-pronged treatment regimen to manage her depression. In her case, she takes an antidepressant medication, attends weekly group therapy, and uses conflict resolution techniques to deal with interpersonal conflicts with family members or friends. In the past, there were quite a few dark days. Her parents can recall when Betty would stay in bed for an entire week, even though her parents tried to coax her to eat some soup, play a game of spades, or watch a video.

Then there were the times when she would use alcohol and illegal drugs in an attempt to alleviate her feelings of sadness and anxiety. Her use of drugs and alcohol only lasted for 2 years, her seventh and eighth grades, and now she does not use either. There are still some days when Betty remains in her dark bedroom under the covers, refusing to speak to anyone. Betty refers to these days as the "demon days." She jokingly claims to have been possessed by dark demons who steal her spirit. Although she uses this analogy in figurative terms, her mother can't help but notice that part of the demon story seems very real.

Phil and Mill are both glad that Betty is back in school. Although they feel that they have to take some action for Betty's difficulties, they are just happy that Betty is back to "normal." Educated in a regular education classroom, Betty benefits from special consultation services from Norma Gaspin, the special education teacher who works with students with emotional/behavioral disorders. In a unique mainstreaming model, kids with mild disabilities receive almost all of their services in the regular education classroom. Betty tends to do well enough when her mood is up. During depressive cycles, Betty often feels inadequate and unable to keep up with the demands of her classes. Without extra support, she would give up and perhaps even fail. Mrs. Gaspin provides extra emotional support, on-the-spot counseling when Betty feels anxious, and academic tutoring to help Betty prepare for tests. Betty tends to become very anxious before tests. She doubts her own ability to do well on subject matter that she obviously understands. Mrs. Gaspin just provides the little nudge of reassurance that Betty needs to keep her on the right track.

Betty has an IQ slightly above average but often performs on an average level in her academic work. She was also tested for learning disabilities but did not qualify.

For the most part, Betty's parents and Mrs. Gaspin feel that Betty's behavior is like that of most teenagers. Mrs. Drudge, on the other hand, is not in agreement. In the last two meetings with Mrs. Drudge, the first sentence out of her mouth was, "In the twenty years that I have been teaching, I have never had a student quite like Betty." Known for her serious, no-nonsense attitude, Mrs. Drudge annually ranks as one of the most highly rated teachers in the school. She likes to tell parents that she is "tough and effective." She makes students study, complete homework, and take notes—three things, she claims, that too many schools don't teach, resulting in student failure. Unfortunately for Betty, there is a clash between her learning style and the usually successful teaching style of Mrs. Drudge.

Mrs. Drudge has class rules clearly posted on the wall. In plain sight are the following rules: no gum chewing; no talking, unless called upon; no cursing. In addition, all students use "ma'am" and "sir" when addressing adults. The physical layout of her room is such that the desks are arranged in rows, with just enough room between aisles to allow Mrs. Drudge to pass through. Her class schedule is arranged for very little "downtime." Her students are always busy either taking notes from her lectures, completing worksheets, or quietly studying alone. When students are finished working, they must do one of two things: quietly work at one of two content review centers or quietly read their library books. For Betty, sitting still in her seat and being quiet are two skills in which she lacks proficiency.

CASE 23

QUIET FOR JULIA

THE INCIDENT

Julia Whitfield is a twelve-year-old student in the self-contained LD/BD classroom at Washmore Elementary School. It is her first day back in class. She has just returned to school after a 1-month psychiatric hospitalization. As she is walking to the lunchroom with the rest of the class, Larry, another student, runs up behind her and calls her "crazy kid." Two other boys join in with taunts of "looney tunes," "cry baby," and "wacky girl." The boys have heard of Julia's psychiatric problems and have placed a bet to see which student will be the first to make her cry. Finally, after hearing someone whisper to her that her mother made her crazy, Julia begins to cry and bolts ahead of the class. By the time Mrs. Babson, the teacher, catches up to Julia, she is already in full tears and near hysteria. As Mrs. Babson sits down next to her, Julia again gets up and runs to another seat, all the while refusing to talk about what has happened.

BACKGROUND INFORMATION

Julia returned to school after a month-long stay at the residential treatment center known as Quiet Haven. Quiet Haven serves children and adolescents with psychological disorders. In Julia's case, she is recovering from a severe depression. Now stable, the psychiatrists at Quiet Haven feel that she should return to her regular school.

She was originally admitted to Quiet Haven shortly after Christmas because her mother said that she was constantly talking about death and suicide. Julia's mother, Celia Whitfield, noticed that Julia had lost interest in school and social events in early December. Normally, Julia loves the Christmas season. Typically, Julia and a number of her friends would spend the evenings at the arcade in the mall, where the discussions often centered around boys. However, this December was different. Gone were Julia's friends and her normally joyous mood. Instead, Celia observed Julia to be quite irritable and melancholy. When Celia would ask her daughter what was wrong, Julia would reply, "Nothing," or "Leave me alone." After school, Julia would frequently lock herself in her room and listen to her CDs. As the Christmas season passed, Celia noticed no improvement in Julia; in fact, her daughter seemed to be slipping deeper and deeper into depression.

When Celia would ask her husband, "What has happened to our daughter?" Bill, who is an executive with a giant oil company, would simply shrug his shoulders and say that it was part of growing up. Having worked long hours to provide for his family's upper-class lifestyle, Bill has never been very involved in Julia's life. Being the vice president of a major corporation has left Bill with very little time in the evening to speak to or see his daughter. On weekends, Bill generally can be found in front of their large-screen TV watching sports. Bill often admits that his relationship with Julia is at best strained and that he has difficulty talking to her. He remarks, "She talks about girl things. I don't know anything about that stuff."

One of Julia's best friends, Stephanie, stopped by the day after Christmas to listen to some CDs and to drop off a gift for Julia. When Stephanie rang the door bell, Celia answered and was happy to see Stephanie.

"Oh, what a wonderful Christmas surprise!" Celia remarked upon greeting her at the door. She called out to Julia that Stephanie was here to see her, then she whispered in Stephanie's ear that Julia had been feeling down in the dumps recently. As Julia walked down the steps to greet her friend, it was clear that Stephanie's visit was more of an annoyance than a surprise for Julia.

"Why don't you two girls go to your room to spend some time together," Celia said. Once in Julia's room, Stephanie began to quiz her about her erratic behavior. "Why don't you return my calls?" "Why are you acting so weird?" "Why are you always locked up in your room?" These were the first three questions that Stephanie fired at Julia. To each question, Julia had a blank look on her face and replied that she didn't want to deal with people.

Realizing that she had irritated Julia, Stephanie turned the conversation to a new topic. "So Julia, what are you going do for the holidays?" asked Stephanie.

To this Julia replied, "I'm going to see Grandpa Joe."

"Oh, you mean, like, his grave?"

"Yeah."

Stephanie sensed that something wasn't right. She inquired further about Julia's deceased grandfather. "What are you going to do that for?"

"Because I wonder what it would be like, you know, to be dead," replied Julia. Julia and Grandpa Joe were very close and would often spend hours talking about school, friends, and life. When Grandpa Joe died 5 months ago, Julia was very upset, but she seemed to adjust. Throughout their conversation, Stephanie felt uneasy. She wanted to leave but felt compelled to stay. Finally, Stephanie herself was beginning to feel down in the dumps. She abruptly said she had to go home. As Stephanie was leaving the house she remarked to Celia, "That's not the same Julia I knew a month ago."

As Celia closed the door, she too remembered happier times. She recalled how she and Julia used to spend hours hiking in the nearby forest and talking about school. She also recalled how Julia used to love helping her cook and how their conversations would linger well into the evening. Contemplating the changes that she saw in Julia, Celia also felt guilty that she may have inadvertently done something wrong to affect Julia's mood. "Was she too nosy about Julia's problems?" "Was she being too pushy with Julia?" Celia thought to herself.

The house was quiet. Celia caught the sound of Julia's voice. As she listened intently she could hear Julia crying. Immediately, Celia ran to the top of the steps and called out, "Julia, sweetie, is everything okay?" Julia did not respond. As Celia got closer to Julia's locked door, she called out for Julia to open the door so that they could talk. When Julia refused, Celia opened the door and found her daughter sitting in the dark crying.

"Sweetie, you need help," Celia replied. At this, Julia began to cry louder and yell out that she wished that she were dead. Celia told Julia that they were going to see some doctors who could help her. That night they drove to Quiet Haven and admitted Julia.

During her stay at Quiet Haven, Julia met some new friends and began to show improvement. Over the course of a week, she was diagnosed by the staff, and Dr. Chall prescribed the antidepressant drug Prozac. He prescribed it to Julia because of her thoughts of suicide, fatigue, changes in sleep, and lack of appetite. As the day neared for Julia's discharge from Quiet Haven, Dr. Chall informed the parents that Julia was still very fragile and warned them to reduce any stress in Julia's life. "Don't force her to do any activity that she does not want to do. It is only over time in a very supportive environment that Julia will fully recover."

CASE 24

FRUSTRATED BY MATH

THE INCIDENT

Robert sat at his desk muttering to himself, "I don't wanna do this. I don't wanna do this." When Mr. Doyle looked up from his desk to see what he was doing, Robert let out a loud yell and banged on the desk. Robert was supposed to be completing a worksheet of 20 addition problems. Instead he was scribbling cartoon skulls on his paper.

Mr. Doyle went to Robert's desk and tried to redirect him back to his worksheet. "Now, come on Robert. You can answer these problems," he said as he pointed to the worksheet.

Robert let out a yell, "I don't wanna work on this, and you can't make me." With that, the other students let out a simultaneous "Ooohhh."

Mr. Doyle, who was becoming visibly agitated, said, "Look, get to work or you get to go to the corner." Robert sat in his seat motionless, overcome with stubbornness. As Robert was contemplating his limited options, Mr. Doyle snapped at the other students, "Get back to work." Next, he looked at Robert and said firmly, "Get to work." Again, he waited a minute to see what Robert was going to do, and when he saw no movement from Robert, he directed him again to get to work. Robert did not budge.

"That's it! You lose recess!" Mr. Doyle said as he marched to the board. Once in front of the class, he wrote, in bold letters, *ROBERT—NO RECESS*. With chalk cracking as the teacher wrote, some of the other students chimed, "You're in trouble now." Robert defiantly held up the worksheet and ripped it in half.

BACKGROUND INFORMATION

Eleven-year-old Robert has been categorized as having a mild developmental disability. He currently attends Tannerville Elementary School in downtown Gatesburg. Robert has been in Mr. Doyle's class for 2 years and has caused problems for Mr. Doyle on a number of other occasions. Robert has an earned IQ score of 68 on the Wechsler Intelligence Scale for Children. He has academic deficits in all of the basic skill areas: reading, math, and written language. To complicate matters, Robert has also been identified as having Attention Deficit Hyperactivity Disorder (ADHD) and currently takes Ritalin to help control his attention and hyperactivity.

Robert lives at home with his mother, Daphne, in a nearby apartment. Daphne is very concerned with Robert's progress in school. Mr. Doyle has often told her that he wishes his other students' parents were as involved in their children's education as she is in Robert's. Daphne is familiar with Robert's stubbornness. At home, Robert frequently refuses to complete work for her and often runs away from home for short periods of time when confronted with a distressing problem. Daphne has related to Mr. Doyle that mornings are the most difficult for her. During the morning hours, Daphne spends long periods of time waking Robert and getting him ready for school. Even though he goes to bed early enough, he does not like to go to school. He would rather sleep or watch TV all day. She knows her son well, so it came as no surprise when she received a note that night from Mr. Doyle describing the incident during math. When she spoke to Robert about the incident, he refused to discuss it.

That same evening, Mr. Doyle also pondered Robert's unusual behavior. He asked himself a series of questions: "Did I handle it properly?" "Could I have not gotten so angry?" "Should I have immediately put him in the corner?" Only in his second year of teaching, Mr. Doyle still isn't quite certain how to handle many of his students' problems. He remembers back to his college class in behavior management but draws a blank as to what he could have done differently. A "control freak" at heart, Mr. Doyle likes a quiet, orderly, business-like classroom. In the past, he has been able to manage many of the inappropriate behaviors that his students have exhibited, but Robert's behavior has consistently become worse as the school year has progressed.

As the only special education teacher in the school, Mr. Doyle feels that he has to "walk on eggshells" around the principal and other teachers. The principal, Mrs. Gunnison, has a no-nonsense type of management style. She is the type of administrator who would rather suspend a student than seriously discuss the reasons for a student's inappropriate behavior. Mr. Doyle was chosen as the very first special education teacher at Tannerville Elementary School because of his diplomatic style while conferring with other teachers. He was told by his special education supervisor that he needs to establish a good working relationship with the other faculty so that they can try to add other special education classes in the school.

The day after the above incident, Mr. Doyle decided to discuss Robert's behavior with his classroom aide, Kelly Stellar. As they discussed the incident, Kelly told him that Robert had gotten into a heated discussion with another student on the playground immediately prior to coming to math class. In her description of the playground incident, it was Jacob, a rather intimidating boy from another class, who had sparked the quarrel.

In Kelly's words, here's how it happened: "Robert was playing nicely with another student when he was suddenly hit with a red playground ball. As Robert picked up the ball, Jacob started lashing out at Robert, insulting him and telling him that he was interfering in the game. When Jacob went back to his game, Robert appeared to calm down. But, when I asked him to line up, he angrily mumbled something and slowly walked over to the line. Once inside, as we were walking down the hall, I could tell that he was upset about something. He wouldn't talk to me. He just threw his coat angrily into the closet and stormed off to his desk."

CASE 25

GO TO THE OFFICE

THE INCIDENT

A straight and silent row of second graders walked down the right side of the long hallway toward the computer lab. Rashid El-Amin, the tallest boy, walked at the front of the line, his shiny black hair serving as a guiding beacon for the well-trained group of youngsters who obediently followed his lead. Mrs. Topfield strode along at the left shoulder of the fifth student. While her students faced forward with their shoulders square, Mrs. Topfield constantly twisted her torso around to survey the rear two thirds of the line.

A flutter of laughter was emitted from the rear of the line. This was followed by mumbled words and another full giggle. Mrs. Topfield spun around in time to see that it was Kit and Jamal. As is typical of such situations, the teacher did not witness the entire sequence of events but quickly pieced together the scenario based on the evidence available. The first giggle of laughter was Kit. Jamal was standing behind her in the line. Based on previous interactions between the two, Mrs. Topfield could reasonably guess that Jamal had probably poked Kit in the shoulder, tugged her hair, or stepped on the back of her sneakers.

When Mrs. Topfield first spun around, she saw Kit turning to push Jamal's right hand away. The small girl was walking backward and holding her arms in front of her in a defensive stance. The horseplay was obviously not mean spirited on the part of either child. Both students were smiling. Jamal continued in the game for a moment, his hands held up before him as if he were about to tickle Kit. Upon seeing that his teacher was approaching, Jamal started to lower his hands and retreat from the situation. Just then, Kit, who had been walking backward in order to face Jamal, stumbled over the foot of the child in front of her. She let out a tiny shriek, caught herself with one hand as she fell into the wall, and giggled at her own clumsiness.

"Stop! Line leader, stop please!" called Mrs. Topfield. At the front, Rashid halted, and the line instantly froze. Mrs. Topfield walked back toward Jamal and Kit at the rear of the line. She reached one hand forward to help Kit regain her balance. In a moment, both Kit and Jamal were back in line, standing like soldiers with stern faces and straight shoulders.

"What is the positive expectation about walking in the hallway?" the teacher quizzed her class. A hand shot up from the center of the line. Mrs. Topfield called on the boy to respond.

"Single file, head behind the head in front of you, and——" the little boy's voice trailed off as he tried to recall the third aspect of the expectation.

"And?" Mrs. Topfield prompted him in a soft, encouraging voice.

Five other hands flew up. Mrs. Topfield shook her head, and four of the five fell right back down.

"And silent?" the responding boy finally queried in a small voice.

"Yes, Timothy, you are right," Mrs. Topfield praised the boy, handing him a small piece of green paper called a ticket. The boy gladly pocketed the ticket. The teacher then instructed her class on the complete expectation: "We walk in single file. We keep our head behind the head in front of us. We are silent. Alright, Rashid, turn about. Return to the classroom and we'll give this another try."

Rashid crossed the hallway to the opposite side and led the silent line of students back toward their classroom. The students knew that they would then have another attempt at walking to the computer lab according to schoolwide positive expectations.

Mrs. Topfield's students walked quietly and sadly back to their classroom, knowing that they might be losing valuable time in the computer lab. Jamal playfully slipped his foot under Kit's leg, tripping her up slightly at each step. Kit played along, jumping over Jamal's sneaker as though she were dodging cracks in the sidewalk. As the two students entered their classroom, Jamal's foot finally struck Kit firmly on the shin. Their legs tangled together and the boy and girl fell to the ground with a shriek and a gasp.

BACKGROUND INFORMATION

Lanacre Elementary School (K-5), housed in a small building, is located in a suburban school district. Mrs. Topfield's actions in the aboved incident followed the school guidelines that were instituted within the Positive Expectations Program (PEP) 6 months earlier. The principal had called in a university consultant due to concerns with the high number of office referrals for instances of inappropriate behavior. The school of approximately 400 students had accumulated an astounding 1400 office behavior referrals over the course of the previous year. This was a mean of 7.8 office referrals per school day. From the data, it could be determined that a relatively small group of students (22) received a large share of the referrals (74%). Additionally, a small group of three teachers produced over half (56%) of the referrals. Mrs. Topfield's referral figures were slightly below average in comparison to the other teachers.

The principal and consultant decided to view this as a broad systemic issue rather than a problem specific to a few students or a handful of teachers. It was agreed that the intervention should include all students. The consultant emphasized that such an intervention could be immediately instituted without a full investigation into the reasons why teachers were sending students to the office in such numbers. This lack of understanding of the roots of the problem concerned the principal, but she agreed nonetheless to move forward with the consultant's intervention plan.

The university consultant suggested the school utilize PEP, a schoolwide system of positive reinforcement designed to clarify the behavioral expectations of the faculty and train the children to follow the expectations. The consultant, school principal, and faculty met a number of times to develop a short but comprehensive list of behavioral expectations for all students. Following are the five behavioral expectations that resulted from the meetings:

1. **F**ollow teacher directions.
2. **O**nly positive touching is allowed.
3. **U**se respectful language.
4. **R**aise your hand before speaking.
5. **B**e silent in the halls and cafeteria.

These guidelines quickly became known by students and teachers as the FOURB. "Follow the FOURB" became the buzz phrase around the hallways of Lanacre.

During the first 2 months of the school year, the teachers continuously repeated and encouraged the five expectations. Small green tickets were handed out as positive reinforcers to students observed following any one of the five expectations. Students accumulated the tickets and traded them on every second Friday for special privileges and activities such as computer game time or a popcorn and video afternoon. After the first 2 months, the tickets were no longer given to students. Teachers continued to praise students who complied with the rules, but no tangible incentives were offered. By design, the school went 3 months without the tickets. Then the teachers brought the reinforcers back for use during the month of February. This was designed to work like a booster shot, a brief refresher course on the FOURB, encouraging students to again focus on following the behavioral expectations.

Following are the per day averages of office referrals over the first 6 months of the school year:

September (tickets used)—6.1

October (tickets used)—4.4

November (no tickets)—3.9

December (no tickets)—4.5

January (no tickets)—3.5

February (tickets used)—4.0

As of late February, the date when the line behavior incident detailed above occurred, the faculty of Lanacre were generally satisfied with the results of the program and wished to continue.

When the PEP was initially presented to the faculty by the consultant, reactions varied. Most of the teachers were pleased to have a concrete program that outlined very precisely what they should do. The authority and expertise of the university consultant brought an air of likely success to the proposed program. This supportive group retained still a pragmatic ounce of skepticism, a "wait and see how it works" attitude, while generally embracing the program. Mrs. Topfield was one of the "wait and see" teachers.

A small group of teachers made up a rather silent opposition force that did not openly criticize the program in faculty meetings but spoke at length among themselves. This coalition was made up of a trio of teachers who were uncomfortable with the PEP for philosophical reasons. This trio felt that the PEP was too much of a training model that valued an unquestioned form of obedience and uniformity. They sarcastically called the program the "Nineteen Eighty Four B," after the Orwell novel about a frightening future society of absolute conformity.

Kit and Jamal, the two students involved in the line incident, had responded to the program in very different ways. Jamal had always been a pretty well-behaved student, a child who occasionally fooled around behind the teacher's back but always stayed out of serious trouble. He had never been sent to the office for misbehavior. In contrast, Kit was a very active and verbal child who had originally ranked 15th among students in office referrals. Mrs. Topfield found that Kit often became angry and talked back when verbally reprimanded or corrected. When the PEP incentive system was implemented in September, Jamal quickly became one of the highest ticket earners in the school, while Kit earned very few tickets. Mrs. Topfield made a special effort to reward Kit with a ticket for the most meager demonstration of meeting the behavioral expectations. Her ticket totals soared through the month of October. Nonetheless, Kit's office referral numbers dropped only slightly over the 6 months. It was evident that the PEP was having an uneven impact on Kit's behavior.

A specific group of students seemed to be untouched by the program. While the schoolwide referral figures dropped significantly, 18 of the 22 students who had been sent to the office most frequently during the prior year continued to receive office referrals at the same high rate.

CASE 26

OFF TASK

THE INCIDENT

Mr. Palatino rubbed his hands together nervously. He glanced up at Mrs. Sanchez, his co-teacher. She smiled hesitantly across the classroom. Both knew what was on the line. Their supervisor, Principal Estes, was seated at the front of the room with a state-mandated effective teaching evaluation instrument in her hands. The key to her evaluation of their classroom came down to "time on task," the amount of time the students spent actually working on their academic activities, a frequent weakness among the students in the Palatino-Sanchez inclusion class.

Mrs. Estes was observing the sixth-grade inclusion class, a pilot program developed by Mr. Palatino and Mrs. Sanchez. The two veteran teachers knew that Mrs. Estes was a stickler for the old-school teaching style. The students had to be on task, heads down, working on their assignments. This was exactly the difficulty that the Palatino-Sanchez class was experiencing. Mr. Palatino had just finished leading the class in an oral introduction to the social studies lesson. He spoke for 5 minutes, about 3 minutes longer than the students seemed to listen. Their eyes wandered, and a few whispered private comments to their neighbors. Then, as the students turned to page 24 and started on the individual reading and writing in their workbooks, the two teachers circled the room in a constant effort to keep the eyes down and the pencils moving. Despite their physical proximity and their gently spoken prompts to the students, Mrs. Estes could see that at any given moment, half of the children were off task. They were silent, but their eyes and minds were wandering from the work at hand. Seeing this, and feeling the pressure of the observation, the two teachers redoubled their efforts, encouraging all to complete the reading assignment and the written activities.

After the lesson, Mrs. Estes commented briefly that the air conditioning system was too loud and distracting. Mrs. Sanchez agreed, but she took little heart in this excuse.

BACKGROUND INFORMATION

Principal Estes and the faculty of Sennett Center recently came under fire from the central district offices because they were the only school in their small rural district that had not developed at least one inclusion classroom. Mrs. Sanchez was teaching a self-contained, cross-categorical special education class for students diagnosed with mild degrees of various disabilities: mental retardation, learning disabilities, and behavior disorders. She and Mr. Palatino had discussed the creation of a team-taught, inclusion classroom with Mrs. Estes 2 years earlier. Mrs. Estes was very skeptical about the idea. She had heard the hype and the hoopla about inclusion at a number of educational conferences, but she was very suspicious of reform movements. She had seen them come and go over the years. In the end, she was convinced that it always came back to business as usual in her school. She felt that the pull-out model was best for her exceptional students. It had been working fine during her 14 years at the helm. She could see no reason to create an uproar simply because some overly idealistic people behind central administration desks didn't know the realities of educating students with disabilities.

When the superintendent finally gave Mrs. Estes no choice, she reluctantly told Mrs. Sanchez to move her 11 special needs students into Mr. Palatino's room on a full-time basis. On the first day of school, the superintendent himself was present for the inauguration of the program. He encouraged the two teachers and told them to seek the support of his office if they needed any information or special help. The two teachers, knowing little about team teaching and inclusion beyond the few articles they had read about inclusive programs elsewhere, knew that they were initiating a mixed blessing. Supposedly, they had the full support of the fairly inaccessible superintendent's office. They knew he was cheering for them, but he had offered them no special training in preparation for the venture. Meanwhile, they knew that their own Principal Estes would undoubtedly be watching them with a skeptical eye, looking for an opportunity to demonstrate the ineffectiveness of the inclusion model. Needless to say, the two teachers felt enormous pressure.

The one sure benefit of the superintendent's endorsement was that Mr. Palatino and Mrs. Sanchez were allowed to interview prospective students' parents before placing the students in the class, in order to guarantee full parental support for the inclusion program. Before the school year began, the two teachers met with every parent to explain the program and to hear their hopes and misgivings. They interviewed all the students' parents, working under the principle that participation in the special program must be voluntary. No parents would be forced to put their child in their class. They arrived at the final group of 25 students, 14 general education and 11 exceptional education students.

The class was as eclectic a group of children as one could find in this relatively homogeneous rural school. The local population was over 95% white; it consisted of farmers, factory workers, and a sprinkling of Mexican migrant worker families that typically moved about as the various crops required. The inclusion class was populated with general education third graders and special education students who ranged from third grade to fifth grade. The class was balanced in terms of gender. The general education group had six Mexican students with limited English proficiency. Both Mrs. Sanchez and Mr. Palatino spoke passable Spanish and felt able to work with these students.

The special education contingent was made up of all boys who had spent the previous years in a self-contained special education class at the elementary school. They had become comfortable with both each other and the small, segregated setting.

In the first 2 months of school preceding Mrs. Estes' evaluation, Mrs. Sanchez and Mr. Palatino had already identified a series of major problems needing their attention. First of all, the two teachers have very different teaching styles. Mr. Palatino tends to run a pretty traditional classroom. Students sit in rows, and the teacher leads whole-class lessons from the front of the room. Students are expected to follow his oral explanations and instructions as he introduces a new concept or skill. Often he writes on the board as he explains or gives directions. This teacher-directed content is typically followed by individual practice activities that students complete using workbooks, worksheets, or their texts.

In contrast, while teaching in the self-contained special education classroom, Mrs. Sanchez grew accustomed to using small cooperative groups and tutoring dyads for virtually all of her instruction. Given the wide range of reading and math abilities and frequent disinterest or inattention among her students, she has worked hard to design small projects that teams of two to four students can complete in a short period of time. Often these projects have been thematic, integrating math skills and writing or bringing together language arts and science. The thematic nature of the activities has freed up time for Mrs. Sanchez to create curriculum on topics of interest to the students. For instance, she developed an extensive, integrated unit on spiders, an area of mutual intrigue to her pack of preadolescent boys. The difficulty Mrs. Sanchez experienced in using this approach was that developing group projects for her students often took incredible quantities of her time.

Mrs. Sanchez and Mr. Palatino have discussed adding more cooperative group work to their inclusion class day. Mr. Palatino has agreed in principle, but he has understandably hesitated to change the format that he has used for years. Given the evident attention problems of the students, he wonders if a new cooperative grouping approach will only further distract the children. "Won't the cooperative group members just distract each other?"

Additionally, since the inclusion class is located in the room that has long been Mr. Palatino's class, Mrs. Sanchez has struggled to feel that the new inclusion class is actually her class. She often feels like a guest, a welcome guest, but a guest nonetheless. Despite the positive working relationship she and her co-teacher share, she is not yet sure to what extent she can suggest and create changes in what still feels like Mr. Palatino's room.

CASE 27

THE ART OF FAIR PLAY

THE INCIDENT

The enormous sliding walls had been pulled across the basketball court, splitting the gymnasium of Tryon Middle School into two somewhat separate rooms. The double gym echoed with the deafening mixture of shouts from the seventh-grade girls playing crab soccer on one side and the sixth-grade boys playing kickball on the other. To the uninitiated newcomer, the sound alone was overwhelming.

The boys' kickball game had been under way for 15 minutes without incident; then a conflict erupted between Ben and Chris. Ben Kidwell was a runner on second base when a hot squibbler was booted into short left field. As Ben ran to third, he accidentally ran into Chris Kelly, the shortstop for the opposing team. Ben and Chris fell to the floor in a heap. The left fielder scooped up the red kickball and tagged Ben out. Ben hopped to his feet and shouted angrily at Chris, who lay stunned on the floor.

"Jeez, Kelly, what'd you get in my way for?" shouted Ben. Chris jumped up quickly and clenched his fists. Ben seemed surprised by the fact that Chris stood up for himself. Chris was usually a fairly passive and meek boy. Ben took a cautious step back.

Mr. Kishna, the physical education teacher, shouted across the gym, "Come on, Ben. Clear the field. You're out. He nailed you fair and square."

Ben walked slowly toward the sideline, seemingly accepting Mr. Kishna's direction. The red kickball had rolled to the sideline and now rested against the bleachers. As Ben reached the bleachers, he picked up the ball and hurled it back onto the field. The ball soared over the pitcher's outstretched hands and struck the unsuspecting Chris Kelly on the side of the face. Chris knew who threw it. He turned and began to stride quickly toward Ben. Chris raised his fists and shouted, "Come on, Kidwell. I've had it with you!"

BACKGROUND INFORMATION

After 18 years of trying to run two physical education classes side by side in a cramped gym, Mr. Kishna and his physical education department colleagues finally thought they were going to get the athletic facilities that Tryon Middle School needed. A recent bond referendum in the small town of Tryon had apparently raised enough money for the new athletic complex, complete with two full gymnasiums. However, a lawsuit had been filed by opponents of the referendum, leaving the issue and Mr. Kishna's hopes of developing a quality physical education program in limbo for months. The veteran coach seemed disheartened. Instead of participating in the games and activities with his middle school students, he had taken to sitting quietly on the sidelines. He had regressed from enthusiastically teaching athletic skills to merely tossing a ball on the court and watching from a distant chair.

Unbeknownst to Coach Kishna at the time of the kickball game, the conflict that erupted between Ben and Chris had roots in earlier interactions between the two boys. Two days prior to this incident, Ben and Chris occupied seats in the front office, each waiting a turn to speak to Mr. Cole, the assistant principal, about unrelated disciplinary matters. Of the two boys, Ben was far more comfortable with being sent to the office. Due to his often disruptive behavior in class and on the bus, he was a veteran of many disciplinary meetings in his 6 short years of schooling.

On the other hand, Chris was unaccustomed to getting into any trouble at all. This was the first time he had ever been sent out of class for misbehavior; he had been sent to the office for fooling around too much in science class. While Ben felt a certain pride in being sent to the office one more time, Chris felt ashamed. He worried that his parents would find out. He shivered and shook like a choir boy riding a prison bus. Sensing Chris's feelings of humiliation, Ben began picking on him. He played on Chris's fear and sadness and tried to make him fear the assistant principal all the more.

"Whatchoo up for, Kelly?" Ben asked as the two waited on the bench outside Mr. Cole's office.

"I was just making jokes. I wouldn't do it again," Chris confessed with a guilty sigh.

"Jokes, huh?" Ben shook his head from side to side. "You know what old man Cole does to jokers?"

"No. What's he do?"

"All I can say is, I wouldn't want to be you. That's all."

Chris's anxiety level began rising like flood waters during the monsoon season. "Why? What do you mean? He's got to be fair. I mean, they got a law about him having to be fair."

"Fair?" Ben laughed and leaned back with a smile. He stuck a pencil in his mouth and pretended to smoke a cigarette. "Cole's got his own idea of fair."

"Like what? Tell me what you mean."

"Well, for one thing, Cole's not running a court or nuthin'. He knows you're guilty even before he talks to you. Second, he calls your mother, tells her all about what you done, playin' it up like it's much worse than the real thing. He gets her crying by telling her that this will be 'a permanent mark on Chris's record.' That's how he puts it. He gets her all crying like you're on your way to leading a life of crime. Then he makes you apologize to her over the phone. You ever try to apologize to your Mom while she's crying hysterically?"

Ben had worked him up into such a frenzy that by the time Chris sat down in the assistant principal's office, he was crying like a baby. It took Mr. Cole 15 minutes to convince Chris that nothing bad would happen to him.

Indeed, Mr. Cole did not call Chris's mother. He talked briefly to Chris about his behavior in science class, encouraging him to keep up his usual hard work and positive attitude, and sent him on his way. As he walked past the grinning Ben, who was still waiting outside the office, Chris realized that he had been hoodwinked. Ben had played him for a fool. Chris shot an angry look at Ben and wondered what he could do to get even.

CASE 28

SIDE BY SIDE

THE INCIDENT

Jim and Steven are 3-year-old boys playing in the sandbox. Each pushes a yellow truck through the thick sand, around his own legs, over molehills, and along the wooden rail that encloses the sand. The boys aren't really playing together. They seem to be playing side by side, making engine sounds in unison, but otherwise keeping their truck-driving activities separate.

There are three other youngsters on the small playground of the Happy Times Preschool, a special program for young children with disabilities or developmental delays. Two children are standing at the back fence, staring curiously and fearfully at a mound of crawling ants that has sprung up over the weekend. They step on the moving mound and jump back with little shouts of exuberance. The fifth student is Josh, a 4-year-old youngster who suffered a severe brain injury as an infant. He does not speak or seem to understand any language. He sits alone, curled up in a semi-fetal position, on the bench just outside the classroom door. He rocks slightly, sucks his thumb, and hums to himself.

Ellen Palliser, the teacher, and Pam Hsu, the classroom aide, are rushing about, attending to the million and one details of Monday morning arrival time. Ellen is standing at the front curb by the entrance, greeting parents and children as they pull up. This morning she is helping Dr. Sanchez try to operate the wheelchair lift on her van so that her daughter Tina can roll off the van and into the school. Dr. Sanchez struggles with the awkward mechanism. It is her husband's van, and she doesn't know how to work the lift. Mr. Sanchez usually delivers Tina to school, but he is home in bed with the flu, leaving Ellen and Dr. Sanchez to figure out how to get Tina off the van.

Pam, feeling rushed by the sudden arrival of her students, moves quickly back and forth between the small playground and the classroom. She is attempting to monitor the students who are entering the classroom and the five already on the playground. She tries to rush the arriving students out onto the playground so that she will only have to monitor one area. The students move slowly, so for now she is stuck with watching children in two places at once. With each hurried pass through the open doorway, she briefly rubs little Josh on the head, attempting to briefly console him. He looks like he could use some comfort. On Monday mornings he often cries and screams as his mother leaves him with his teachers and drives away. He seems to go through a new separation process every week. Pam can't wait until she gets a few minutes to sit with him, hold him, and sing him a song. That usually does the trick.

Back in the sandbox, Jim accidentally runs his truck over Steven's hand. Without hesitation, Steven smashes his truck into the rear of Jim's truck. Steven laughs. Jim pulls his hand away, as if frightened. He turns his back to Steven and plays with his truck on the opposite side of the sandbox. Steven then rams his truck into Jim's back. A look of pain comes across Jim's face. As Steven winds up to land another blow, Jim says, "No," and reaches out his hand to try to stop the truck from hitting him again. Steven swings the truck forcefully, crashing through Jim's fingers and opening a small cut on the palm of his hand. Jim sees the blood and starts to cry.

"'Tupid," says Steven in response to Jim's crying.

Pam Hsu has seen this incident from the doorway, where she had paused to tickle Josh. She rushes across the playground to intervene.

BACKGROUND INFORMATION

Ellen has noticed that Steven's maternal grandparents have dropped him off and picked him up for 4 days in a row. Ellen already knew that Steven's parents are embroiled in a very difficult divorce, including a bitter and expensive struggle for custody of Steven and his older sister Rachel. Although Steven's mother has temporary custody of the children, they have recently been staying with their grandparents while she is away on a business trip to Japan. One afternoon last week, both Steven's father and his maternal grandmother showed up to pick him up after school. This led to a nasty shouting match between the two on the front steps as other parents and children looked on. Ellen had to explain to Steven's father that she could not release the boy to him because he was no longer the legal guardian. He got into his car and tore out of the parking lot with tires squealing.

Steven was admitted to the special program a year earlier due to a significant delay in language development. His general intellectual functioning is considered to be within the typical range. No specific source for his language delay has been found.

Steven's behavior has grown increasingly angry and violent as his parents' divorce and custody battle has dragged on. Even when his parents were together, Steven was a very boisterous boy who loved to roughhouse and tumble around. He seemed to feed off of physical play. But he accepted limits set by his teachers and seemed to want to please adults. Even if a situation made him angry, he would try to follow Pam's or Ellen's directions. But in recent days, he has been so angry that he doesn't seem to care very much about how others feel or what others say.

Additionally, when Ellen has tried to talk to Steven's mother about his behavior, she has found her to be very distant and detached. She doesn't seem to want to hear about Steven's difficulties in following directions or getting along with the other children. She seems far away, overwhelmed with other issues, as if one more straw on the camel's back would be too much.

Ellen and Pam have been struggling with some problems of their own. Ellen is a veteran preschool teacher who has taught at Happy Times Preschool for 10 years. Two years ago, the school district went through a dramatic restructuring and suddenly changed Happy Times to a special education preschool. Ellen was very upset by this program change. She had virtually no experience and even less confidence with youngsters with disabilities. The district attempted to comfort her by supplying her with Pam Hsu, a classroom aide who is both certified and experienced in early childhood special education. Pam accepted the low-paying aide position because she was new to the area and there were no other special education preschool teaching openings in the district.

Ellen is just now taking some of the university courses necessary to obtain early childhood special education certification. Her employer gave her 2 years to add this certification. Ellen procrastinated for a year by not taking any classes. Now she is worried that if she doesn't complete her certification on time, the district will hand the Happy Times teaching position to Pam. Silently, and with a fair amount of guilt, Pam hopes to become the teacher at Happy Times.

Needless to say, this has caused a fair amount of tension between the two direct service professionals at Happy Times. Although both teachers are fully aware of this issue and the growing tension between them, the problem has been swept under the rug. As a result, their communication is now minimal and barely cordial. Much like little Steven and Jimmy in the sandbox, Pam and Ellen tend to work side by side but not really together.

Three weeks ago they received the annual program evaluation report written by Dr. Sara Singh, the district supervisor overseeing Happy Times and a handful of similar early childhood programs. In this evaluation report Dr. Singh wrote:

> Professional communication, a necessity in serving children and their families, has deteriorated in recent months. At times, the classroom is noticeably tense and uncomfortable, possibly influencing the children in ways beyond my observations. In my four hour observation on April 18, the teacher and aide spoke to each other three times. On interview, neither Ms. Hsu or Ms. Palliser

could offer any reasons why they are not talking to one another. Lacking substantial understanding of the source of the discord, I can merely note that this is an unfortunate decline in communication at a site that has previously been exemplary in all respects. I spoke individually with both Ms. Hsu and Ms. Palliser and encouraged them to improve the communication concerning professional issues.

CASE 29

SKIPPING

THE INCIDENT

"Christy, you can come out for dinner!" Mr. Cleveland called down the hallway. There was no response. An hour earlier, after a loud argument between the father and 13-year-old daughter, Mr. Cleveland sent Christy to her room. Mr. Cleveland had just received a phone call from Mr. Hodapp, Christy's math teacher, informing him that his daughter had already failed math for the quarter due to excessive absences. Mr. Cleveland was shocked and angered. For weeks, Christy had been skipping her math classes, which took place during the final period of the day.

"Christy! Did you hear me?" Mr. Cleveland shouted impatiently. Hearing no reply, he walked quickly down the hallway and knocked on Christy's door. There was no answer. He opened the door to find the room empty. The open window testified to Christy's escape route.

Mr. Cleveland immediately telephoned Christy's best friend April. When April answered the phone, Mr. Cleveland asked to speak to his daughter. Mr. Cleveland heard the girls' voices in the background, but he couldn't make out what they said to one another. Then April returned to sheepishly pass on a message from Christy.

"She says she can't talk to you right now, Mr. Cleveland. She says she's fine and she'll be home tonight or tomorrow." The line went dead. Mr. Cleveland hung up the phone and sat on the couch to think about the situation.

BACKGROUND INFORMATION

This is the third time Christy has escaped through her bedroom window after being sent to her room. Mr. Cleveland has never believed that sending Christy to her room is an effective disciplinary technique, but it is the only punishment he can think of. The trials of raising an adolescent daughter overwhelm Mr. Cleveland. His little girl is now wearing eye makeup that makes her look like a raccoon, hanging out with ragged-looking boys at the mall, listening to music that sounds like an unending train wreck, and continuously complaining that school is boring.

In the midst of all this, Mr. Cleveland is thankful for the advice and support of Mr. Hodapp, a man who turned out to be not only a good math teacher but also a pretty fair counselor on the exigencies of fathering an adolescent. Mr. Hodapp had demonstrated an early interest in Christy's well-being. At the beginning of the school year, he noticed that Christy had an unusual talent for mathematics, a talent that she seemed to neither notice nor care about. Mr. Hodapp called Mr. Cleveland to suggest that Christy might benefit from joining the Slide Rulers, the math and computer skills club and competition team at the junior high school. Mr. Hodapp has served as faculty sponsor for the club for over 20 years (since the days when the pre-technological moniker wasn't such an anachronism), leading the club to six state titles in math competitions. During this initial discussion, the two men discovered that they had much in common; each was a single parent with a 13-year-old daughter.

Mr. Cleveland looks to the educator for advice in dealing with Christy's behavior problems. Mr. Hodapp emphasizes the need for absolute consistency. Setting a firm list of expectations and then upholding them is the key, according to Mr. Hodapp. He advised Mr. Cleveland to make a list of 10 expectations, those behaviors that Christy must do. For instance, school attendance and completing all homework would be reasonable expectations. Next to each of the expectations, Mr. Hodapp advised, write down the consequence for not meeting the expectation. Consequences should mostly consist of losing privileges and freedoms. Then sit the girl down and explain it all to her. After that, you just have to apply the rules consistently. Mr. Cleveland did exactly this because it seemed to be a logical and sound approach, but he wonders if there isn't more to dealing with his daughter than the dry rationality of enforcing rules.

Mr. Ellis Cleveland and his wife Marjorie separated 8 months before this latest school incident. Their separation has been very stressful and painful for the entire family. Christy is the Clevelands' only child. She lives with her father in a small midwestern town. Her mother lives in a large city an hour and 15 minutes away.

The Clevelands were wed on the day after their high school graduation, over 15 years ago. Ellis took a job at a muffler shop, and Marjorie worked part-time in the dining room of a nursing home. From the start, their relationship was fraught with difficulties. Alcohol abuse and marital infidelity on both sides made for a household of secrets, tension, and conflict.

During the first 9 years of the marriage, Ellis's only sober moments came during the work day. He proved himself to be an able auto mechanic and supervisor, gradually working himself up to shop manager. At home, however, he was frequently drunk, irritable, and verbally abusive to both Marjorie and Christy. It seemed that the more miserable he got, the more he drank, and the more he drank, the more miserable he got.

When Ellis's drinking habit expanded to his work site, his employees at the garage confronted him with his problem. He accompanied a coworker to an Alcoholics Anonymous meeting and started on his recovery. Despite an occasional slip, Ellis has been basically dry for the past 6 years.

Sobriety gave Ellis the sudden ability to see that his marriage was in shambles. He and his wife hardly knew each other. He soon discovered that Marjorie had gone through a string of boyfriends while he had been passed out on the couch in front of the television. Ellis and Marjorie struggled, often arguing late into the night. Their words brought them no resolution; in fact, they only further amplified their feelings of anger and desperation. Marjorie admitted that she had been unfaithful in the past, but she contended that those days were long gone. Ellis wanted to believe her, but he suspected that she continued the affairs. He coped by devoting himself to his work and attending AA meetings almost every evening.

As an only child, Christy often enjoyed the full attention of one or both of her parents. Her father would take her on long hikes in the forest behind their house, hoisting her up on his shoulders to carry her when she tired on the way home. When he carried her, she felt like her father's special girl. Her mother was a talented amateur artist who patiently taught her daughter how to draw. The two spent lazy afternoons sketching rural landscapes filled with barns and covered bridges. While the love between her parents often was lacking, Christy developed very full and rewarding relationships with each of the two adults.

It would be inaccurate to claim that the difficulties between her parents did not confuse Christy. Her father often went on prolonged drinking binges. For weeks his mood would climb to an almost surreal ecstasy, as if he were the king of the world. Then, suddenly, he would dive into a deep depression. Christy learned to recognize the changes in the timbre and the tone of his voice and to know when her father was becoming agitated and unreasonable. She would lock herself in her room and hide under her bed while her father raged at her mother or shouted at the empty living room.

Also contributing to Christy's delicate sense of confusion was the inconsistency of her mother's love. Sometimes her mother was caring and emotionally available to Christy. Other times, she seemed far away, distant and unfeeling. At those moments, she would remain polite and casual but uninvolved, acting more like a temporary roommate than a loving mother. Also during these times, Christy's mother seemed to yearn for independence, for a way to be somewhere else, far from her troubled family. Occasionally, she would stay out all night. Christy would sleep on the couch and wait for her mother to come home. The next morning her mother would breeze in like a harried celebrity on a world tour. Offering no excuses for her absence and no apologies for her insensitivity, she would gather up a few things and rush off again.

Christy is an eighth-grade student at Abner Doubleday Junior High School. Until recently, she had always been a solid student, earning A's and

B's in most of her subjects. Throughout the five elementary grades, her teachers generally found her to be agreeable and hard working. As a fifth grader, she won the highly competitive district science fair, defeating entrants from four elementary schools. Last year, when she went into the junior high school, Christy's attitude and effort began to change. The girl who was so proud of her school achievement seemed to avoid the limelight of success. Her grades fell to straight C's. When her father asked her why her grades had dropped, Christy shrugged and said, "I'm not into the honor roll anymore, Dad. That stuff's for little kids and nerds."

Christy's alienation from school and academic achievement was further fueled by her parents' separation. Her parents gave her a week to choose which parent she wanted to live with. She found herself torn. While she leaned toward living with her father, she feared insulting and rejecting her mother. As the decision day arrived, Christy's mother suddenly declared that she didn't want Christy living with her. She had married too young and had never been on her own. This was her chance to be independent. Christy took this as a terrible rejection. She moved in with her father. She now visits her mother on every other weekend.

CASE 30

SOFT SPOKEN

THE INCIDENT

While most of the small group of high school boys begin to work on their individual mathematics assignments, Mrs. Rojas notices that neither Norm nor Rico have opened their books. Norm is tilting back nonchalantly in his seat and humming a song under his breath. Rico is bent over as if working on the math problems, but he is grinning and his eyes are fixed on Norm. Mrs. Rojas says: "Now is the time to work on your assignments. If you don't work, you won't earn your points toward Friday's pizza party."

"I got your points, bitch," Norm mumbles in a voice barely audible to the teacher.

"Excuse me, Norm, did you say something?" Mrs. Rojas asks in a puzzled tone. She seems both annoyed and confused by what Norm said.

"No problem here, teacher," Norm states clearly, then his voice trails off, "——stupid bitch." Norm makes these final words somewhat ambiguous to Mrs. Rojas, almost as if he is baiting or teasing her. His insult is very clear to the students sitting near him. All eyes in the room turn first to Norm and then to Mrs. Rojas at her desk. The class is silent and tense.

After 5 seconds of heavy silence, Rico can't stand the tension. "Oh man!" he exclaims. He quickly presses his hand over his mouth to hush his own nervous laughter.

Mrs. Rojas stands up and walks in front of her desk. Her eyes meet Norm's as each wonders what the other will do next.

BACKGROUND INFORMATION

This scene took place in a self-contained special education class for students considered behaviorally disordered. The class is located in the vocational wing of Dwight Evans High School. Mrs. Rojas works with 10 high school students. Next door to her room is a similar class instructed by Mr. Toulouse.

Mrs. Rojas' class has been relatively calm and stable in recent weeks, a far cry from the daily battle of wills that took place from September through November. When she first arrived in the fall, she found that many of her students maintained a great allegiance to their previous teacher. During those first few weeks, it seemed that no matter what Mrs. Rojas did, some student would complain that "Miss Anderson never did it that way." The students were often rebellious and noncompliant. Mrs. Rojas tried to be patient with them. She knew that six of the students had been in Miss Anderson's class for 3 years. These street-tough, hard-talking boys had come to rely on and trust Miss Anderson. Mrs. Rojas knew that it would take time for the students to do the same with her. Gradually, the students began to accept Mrs. Rojas as their teacher. By Christmas, Mrs. Rojas could rightly claim that she had become the teacher of the class.

Mrs. Rojas uses a point/level system of behavior management. Students can earn 1 point per half hour for each of the following general behavior categories:

Following directions

Staying on task

Using good language

Keeping hands and feet to self

Students who tally above 80% of the total possible points on a given day are given a star next to their names on the big wall chart. If a student earns 15 stars, he moves up to the next level. For major rule infractions, such as hitting a peer or leaving an assigned area, students au[...] lose an
entire level. The system has four levels. Students st[...]
the first level and, it is hoped, work their way u[...]
year. As a student moves up the levels, he is gi[...]
activities. Additionally, Mrs. Rojas and Mr[...]
special Friday afternoon activity such as [...]
vidual student must get over 80% of hi[...]
ipate. Those who earn the necessar[...]
activities, and the rest go to M[...]
versa—the two teachers altern[...]
ment manager and taskmaster.

Norm Ferguson is the o[...]
students are scattered evenly [...]
has earned his way up to le[...]
major rule infraction. He h[...]
climbing the levels.

Norm was never in M[...]
have been labeled behavi[...]
grams for most of their s[...]
tion only 3 months prior [...]

During the spring of the prior year, a major change occurred in Norm's life. His parents separated after 22 years of marriage. Norm remains with his mother in the family home; his father lives across town. Soon after the separation, Norm was thrown out of the Thorndike School, a local private academy. He had tapped into the school computer system, accessed the hall locker combinations, and proceeded to steal over $2,000 worth of his peers' personal belongings. When he was finally caught, he attempted suicide with sleeping pills. He spent the summer receiving treatment in a private psychiatric hospital.

Because of his expulsion from Thorndike, other private schools in the area refused to admit him. So, he entered the tenth grade at Dwight Evans High School in September, his first time in a public school. By November, he had been suspended three times for fighting and verbally threatening other students. A number of this teachers told the principal that they and many of the students feared Norm. They referred him for evaluation and possible placement in special education. Despite the fact that Norm's disciplinary record at Thorndike had been spotless for many years, the evaluation committee decided that his recent violent behavior was serious enough to warrant the BD label and placement in Mrs. Rojas's class.

Mrs. Rojas finds Norm to be a very angry, brooding figure who often seems overwhelmed by the power of his own emotions. He has a soft-spoken and kind manner of interaction, yet his words often seem tinged with bitterness and irony. Mrs. Rojas and the school guidance counselor lead group counseling sessions with the boys two afternoons per week. It is evident in these sessions that Norm does not like to discuss himself or his family, preferring to keep his problems to himself. He holds his fiery anger within tense shoulders and a deeply furrowed brow. Mrs. Rojas has found that humor is the best way to work with Norm. She teases him sometimes about being so private with his troubles. He enjoys the teasing and joking.

"Now don't you go telling anybody that you're mad or anything, Norm," she jokes. "You wouldn't want to let anybody know you're human."

Norm chuckles and comes right back at her. "That's 'cause I'm not human, Miz R. I'm a robot sent down by evil aliens. I'm programmed to haunt you for the rest of your days."

Mrs. Rojas laughs and sneaks up to whisper in his ear, "My pleasure."

Through this connection, Mrs. Rojas and Norm had been able to work together. He had no major behavior difficulties in her class prior to the ... related above.

...ena is the boy with the greatest emotional attachment to Miss ...g after his classmates had warmed up to Mrs. Rojas, he ... a day obsessing over his previous teacher's absence. On ...ould tell Mrs. Rojas that she wasn't the real teacher ... take Miss Anderson's place. Mrs. Rojas would try ...d no intention of taking Miss Anderson's place in the students' hearts and minds but that she was the one and only teacher in this classroom.

Rico tends to be an outcast in the class. He typically has no close friendships. Occasionally, he has latched onto a peer, becoming very dependent on that single boy. In recent weeks, Mrs. Rojas has watched Rico follow Norm around the classroom. When the students go to lunch or take a break and play cards, Rico insists on sitting next to Norm. At first, Norm seemed upset by all this attention. Then he seemed to like and take advantage of the attention. He has Rico do favors and run errands for him, clean up his locker, and keep his school supplies stocked. Mrs. Rojas wonders if she should talk to one or both of the boys about their relationship; it appears to her that Norm is using Rico. She isn't sure how either boy would react to such a confrontation.

Adding more fuel to the fire, Mrs. Rojas is aware that the other boys in the class have been passing around stories about Rico and Norm being gay lovers. She has no idea whether there is any truth to this, but she is concerned that the entire matter is getting out of control.

Additionally, Mrs. Rojas is somewhat confused by what she perceives to be mixed messages coming from her principal, Dr. Goldfarb. The principal has tried to be very supportive of the two self-contained BD classrooms, offering to set aside the standard disciplinary policies to handle such matters with students on a case by case basis. This approach supports Mrs. Rojas's belief that each student is unique and should be dealt with in an individualized manner. She also believes that each problem that arises is unique and deserves the problem-solving attention of the professionals. While this flexibility has been helpful to Mrs. Rojas, she also senses that often Dr. Goldfarb becomes annoyed when Mrs. Rojas sends a student to her office with a behavior referral slip. She seems to simply not want to deal with these students if at all possible.

TEACHER-PARENT COLLABORATIONS: THE ART OF WORKING TOGETHER

C A S E **31** 

TALK ISN'T CHEAP

THE INCIDENT

Ms. Lois Sampson, the creative writing teacher, is standing in front of the room lecturing to her students on how to edit their compositions. She directs students to turn to page 53 in their textbooks to follow along as she reads aloud. "It is essential that your completed composition be well edited."

Midway through the sentence, she hears a young voice cry out, "Yo, Keasha, look at this masterpiece." It is Vershon, who is talking to Keasha as he shows her his composition.

Keasha quickly scans the page. Upon seeing her name, she cries out, "Hey, what's my name doing on your paper?" Immediately, Ms. Sampson looks up from her book and glares at Keasha.

At the same time, Vershon whispers, "Girl, keep it quiet." Ms. Sampson finishes reading the sentence and then stops class.

"Do I have to stop class again because someone is talking?" she asks the class. In a chorus of muffled, sleepy voices the students answer, "No."

Talking is the biggest problem that Ms. Sampson is having with her students. Often when she is lecturing at the front of the room, half the students ignore her and talk amongst themselves. The situation is so bad that Mr. Kasaski, the principal, has had to pop in on a number of occasions to quiet the students. In his most recent evaluation of Ms. Sampson, Mr. Kasaski wrote, "It is critical that you work at better classroom management to control the volume level in your classes. This is a problem with serious ramifications." Along with this comment came a "low" rating on the evaluation form. In turn, this meant that she would not receive the large salary increase she had hoped for but instead would again receive low merit pay.

BACKGROUND INFORMATION

Lois Sampson is a second-year teacher at Quigley High School who struggled through her first year of teaching. It was only through the intervention of her mentor, Flo, that Lois was even hired back. The two teachers worked together last year to try to find ways to increase student interest and reduce off-task behaviors, such as talking and goofing around. Flo, a third-year teacher, had observed Lois's classes; she witnessed the students talking out, getting out of their seats, and talking back to Lois. Lois graduated in the top of her college class and received honors for her cumulative average, but upon graduating, her teaching was less than successful. This is evidenced by comments on her first-year evaluation: "Lois is extremely knowledgeable about techniques and strategies. Her 'book knowledge' is indicative of great potential." Indeed, Lois could name many different types of effective teaching and classroom management techniques; however, the techniques often fail because of her poor execution. And while Flo recognizes the errors in Lois's teaching, she is unable to help her remedy them. As Flo put it, "Lois is extremely intelligent, but when it comes to application, she is a million miles away."

Lois often uses nagging to get students to complete assignments and to remain quiet. Her threat of sending them to detention only goes so far. She realizes that many of the students whom she would like to send to detention either work or have to baby-sit their younger siblings after school. For these reasons alone, many of her threats of detention go unfulfilled. On those rare occasions when she sends students to detention, they often sleep through it and/or get sent home early by the detention teacher. And frequently students are sent home because there is no one available to supervise the detention room. Lois often blames the school's inconsistent use of detention ("I have no support") for the inappropriate student behaviors in her class, or she blames poor parenting skills ("Parents just don't care"). She once said to Mr. Kasaski, "The students' behavior is just beyond my control."

Quigley High School is not an easy place for a new teacher to perfect his or her skills. The urban setting repeatedly yields fights, drugs, and a less than secure environment for learning. As you enter Quigley, one of the first things that you notice is the noise level. The plaster walls and tall ceilings amplify voices and sounds. For many alumni, Quigley High School was a place of honor and tradition that held many fond memories. Today, however, the walls are cracked, the books are old, and there are all new faces among the faculty. Mr. Kasaski remembers those glory days and tries to relate that feeling to his current students. But Mr. Kasaski also thinks that today's students represent an entirely new generation of kids who don't often use the words *pride, honor,* and *hard work* in their vocabulary.

Both Keasha and Vershon have been attending Quigley for the past 2 years. They live in the same neighborhood and have been classmates since childhood. Over the years, they have become good friends. In times of trouble, they have always been there for each other. For instance, a few years ago, when Keasha's father came home drunk and began to hit her, it was Vershon who came to her rescue by pushing her father out the house. Likewise, when Vershon lost his younger sister to a drug overdose, it was Keasha who was there to comfort him and get him through the rough times. In high school, both students have excelled and plan to attend college upon graduation, making these two students exceptions to the rule at Quigley. Over the past 10 years in his own neighborhood, Vershon has witnessed beautiful homes with caring neighbors transform into crack houses with nightly police raids. Rather than fall into the trappings of the "big money" from dealing drugs, Vershon and Keasha have sought refuge in their local church to stay on the straight and narrow path. Keasha is active in the choir, and Vershon works with young children in an after-school program.

Despite their talent and their fondness for Ms. Sampson, both students see creative writing class as a joke. They fail to see a relevant connection between creative writing and their career goals. Vershon, who wants to be a chef and restaurant owner, often complains that most of the academic "stuff" in school will not help him in his future. And Keasha, who wants to be a veterinary doctor, often does not complete writing assignments. She has told Ms. Sampson that she "hates" writing. Meanwhile, Ms. Sampson has very few curricular resources at her disposal for students and makes do with decade old books and limited supplies of writing paper. Her class has access to two computers in the library, but the entire school must share them. Lacking ideas and old before her time, Ms. Sampson has considered quitting and working for a book publisher.

CASE 32

TATTLETALE

THE INCIDENT

"Quietly now! Quietly now!" Ms. Stanfield half whispers and half shouts to her fifth-grade class as they noisily fumble with their coats in the closet at the rear of the room. They have just come in from the playground. Mr. Lewis, the paraprofessional who monitors recess, enters with John. Mr. Lewis looks perplexed and tired. His right hand is set firmly on the student's shoulder, holding the youngster in place. John's head hangs low in embarrassment, and he wiggles his shoulders in a halfhearted attempt to free himself from Mr. Lewis's grasp. The paraprofessional marches the youngster up to the teacher at the front of the room.

"Where have you been?" Ms. Stanfield asks John. He stares at his feet in silence.

"He did it again, Ms. Stanfield. This time I found him way out in the forest, a good 200 yards off the playground. He was messing around in the creek," explains Mr. Lewis.

Ms. Stanfield crouches down to John's level and speaks softly, "John, tell me why you ran off."

John keeps his eyes to the floor and mumbles, "Teasing."

"Teasing? They were teasing you again?" asks the teacher. "Who was teasing you, John? You can tell me."

The boy's eyes well up with tears. He rubs his eyes and shakes his head.

"Won't you tell me who teased you?" Ms. Stanfield queries. "If you tell me, I can help you."

John shakes his head vehemently. The other students in the class are now sitting at their desks. They have been watching with great interest.

BACKGROUND INFORMATION

John is a fifth-grade student who is extremely intelligent and very overweight. When he speaks, the words come out garbled and jumbled, sounding as if they had been mashed up and rearranged somewhere between his brain and his mouth. Although John tries to mask this speech impediment by speaking rarely or by whispering, his fellow students are aware of his pronunciation difficulties. He receives speech and language services from a specialist who pulls John out of his class for brief one-on-one sessions; she also provides language development activities for all the students within the general education class. Most of the students find John to be somewhat odd, primarily due to his speech and enormous size but also because of his somewhat obsessive desire to talk about computers and adult books that no one else has read.

John struggles to fit in with the other students during recess. He plays with different groups, never settling in long enough to become a regular. Some days he wanders around alone, circling the periphery of the playground, watching the other children from a distance. Recently he has tried to play with Wendell and Billy, two boys who climb on the giant rocks at the point where the playground meets the woods. They stand on top of the large stones and talk about space travel and science fiction movies. John shares these interests, but he also finds these boys to be somewhat childish when they play with their action figures and make goofy noises. The fact that Wendell and Billy tend to babble on endlessly is a source of both comfort and annoyance to John. He is able to be part of the little group without talking very often. Yet he is also too aware of his role as the third wheel on the bike, a vehicle only somewhat to his liking.

One reason John tends to hang around with Wendell and Billy has little to do with the two boys and their interests. It comes down to location. John knows that these two science fiction chums play over by the big rocks, a place far away from any other group of children. Most importantly, they play at a great distance from the tough boys who often tease John because of his weight and his garbled speech.

When the tough boys first teased John, he immediately told Ms. Stanfield. She punished the boys who had called John names. For the rest of the week, those boys called John a tattletale. To John's surprise, many of the other children did, too. Suddenly the problem of being picked on by a few mean boys had exploded into an enormous situation. John was taunted by kids he didn't even know, including some girls who he thought were nice to everyone. John learned very quickly that he had broken a code of the school yard. Only the weakest child could get away with running to the teacher and telling on somebody. Everyone knew that being a tattletale was even worse than being fat or talking funny.

John decided never to tattle on his classmates again. For the next 2 months, he clung to Mr. Lewis's side as a protection from the tough guys who called him names. Mr. Lewis allowed John to sit by him at recess for a few days, then he began to encourage John to play with his peers. At first, the encouragement came in gentle words. "Wouldn't you rather play ball with the other kids?" Mr. Lewis would ask. "I'm just a boring old man who sits on a bench." After a while, Mr. Lewis became pretty impatient. He pushed John to socialize, ordering him firmly, "Go out there and play with the other children. You're not sitting with me. I'm not your nursemaid." John took the hint and starting playing with Billy and Wendell.

As Ms. Stanfield speaks to John about running away and the way the other children tease him, she is reminded of her discussion with John's parents just a week before. In that parent-teacher conference, Ms. Stanfield listened as John's parents, Jaime and Ed, expressed their concerns about John's difficulties in making friends. They were worried about John becoming an outcast, a loner.

John is the youngest child in the family. His three sisters are more than 10 years older than he. John was a bit of a surprise to Jaime and Ed, who had considered their childbearing years to be long over when they found out a fourth baby was on the way. They welcomed the new addition, but they also found young John to be more of a challenge than their previous three children. Even as an infant, he often seemed dissatisfied, inexplicably sullen, and listless. He was diagnosed with a severe articulation disorder and began receiving speech therapy when he was 4 years old. He has made steady progress, yet he still has a long way to go if his speech is to be understood by people outside his family. Additionally, despite his parents' best efforts to regulate his diet, John has inherited his father's weight problem, a burden that John's sisters somehow escaped.

"Sometimes I just don't know what to do with him," Jaime confessed to Ms. Stanfield. "There are days when he seems resigned to the fact that he won't make any friends. At least 2 days a week he cries and begs me to let him stay home from school."

Additionally, Ms. Stanfield knows that her class this year has not yet become a peaceful and unified group. She has struggled in dealing with a wide range of troubling social dynamics, primarily concerning two groups of students. The team of tough boys who tease John consists of an inner circle of two leaders, Matt and Cedric, and a continuously shifting lineup of three to six other boys who tend to follow the negative leadership of the central two. For the first 2 weeks of the year, Ms. Stanfield heard consistent reports from students that Matt and Cedric were terrorizing their peers in the boys' room and on the long hallway behind the gym. Then the reports suddenly stopped, but not because the intimidation had ended. It seems that everyone had gotten the message not to tell the teacher. Ms. Stanfield has tried to win over the two lead boys by designating them as her special classroom helpers. The boys have obediently completed the various chores assigned to them, but that seems to have had no effect on the many subtle ways they intimidate their peers.

The second group of youngsters that concerns Ms. Stanfield consists of four girls, all hard workers and teacher pleasers. While all four do well in their academics, Ms. Stanfield is worried about the way the girls criticize their peers because of clothing and appearance. The girls are fortunate enough to own and wear expensive designer clothes and shoes to school. They have set a divisive, competitive standard for appearance in the room. At times, they have picked on John and others because of physical characteristics such as size and hair color. Ms. Stanfield has spoken to the girls about their behavior, but their preoccupation with appearance seems firmly entrenched.

CASE 33

TURNING UPSIDE DOWN

THE INCIDENT

The youngsters in Mrs. Grogan's second-grade class quickly hang their jackets and personal items in the closet, sit down quietly at their desks, and begin the day with individual work activities. Chris is an academically able child who has no difficulty handling the set of mathematics review sheets. He squirms about in his seat and knocks his papers and pencil to the floor.

"Chris," Mrs. Grogan calls across the room in a soft voice.

"Yeah?" Chris asks innocently.

"You know."

"Yeah."

As Chris leans over to pick up the fallen items, he spins sideways in his seat like an acrobat, turning the small cleanup task into a prolonged gymnastic exercise. After he has picked up his pencil and papers, he sticks the pencil in his mouth and stares up at the ceiling. He seems to be daydreaming. He chews the pencil eraser with his teeth and spins the pencil with his hand. He accidentally drops the pencil to the floor. In an effort to retrieve the pencil, he sprawls on his stomach, laying across his chair with arms and legs balanced delicately in each direction. Mrs. Grogan walks over to his desk and gently directs him to start his work. He finally retrieves his pencil and starts on an arithmetic problem.

After he finishes the first of three math sheets, Chris spins his little body upside down into a headstand. His rear end sticks upward, his feet dangle onto his desk, and his head is far below on the chair itself. Mrs. Grogan verbally directs Chris to sit up straight, but he does not respond. Many of the other students are becoming distracted by Chris's acrobatics. They are off task and giggling.

BACKGROUND INFORMATION

This is not the first time that Chris has squirmed in his seat, dropped items on the floor, and flipped himself upside down. It seems to Mrs. Grogan that

Chris goes through streaks of good and bad behavior that last for about 2 to 3 weeks. He will sit calm and upright in his seat for a few weeks, completing all of his academic work. Then, for reasons unknown to Mrs. Grogan, he will become increasingly antsy. His entire body will be restless and fidgety. During these squirmy days, he will push the seat away and work standing up. He appears uncomfortable in his own body. The zenith of this hyperactivity occurs when Chris stands on his head.

Mrs. Grogan has tried a number of interventions to help Chris sit quietly at his seat. Most often, she simply provides verbal redirection, telling Chris to sit appropriately at his desk. This seems to have varied effectiveness. Sometimes Chris listens and corrects himself. Sometimes he seems to be oblivious to her directions, behaving as if he didn't hear her or it doesn't matter to him. When he does not respond to repeated verbal redirection, Mrs. Grogan sends him to the time-out chair in the corner of the classroom. Typically, Mrs. Grogan ends up telling Chris to go to time-out three or four times before he responds. Sometimes he stomps off angrily and sulks in the corner. Other times, he seems to be in a sort of daze. He strolls over to time-out wearing a dull, emotionless look on his face. Based on Mrs. Grogan's records, the use of time-out has not reduced the frequency of Chris's headstands.

Mrs. Grogan has recently started to wonder if her best bet isn't simply to put up with Chris's seat behavior and wait for the good, calm weeks to return. She is also aware that Chris's seat behavior often (not always) improves as the school day goes on. For some reason, the initial moments of the morning seem to be the most hyperactive and disorganized.

Mrs. Grogan is a veteran teacher in her 19th year at Southern Elementary School. She has watched the student population of her school change dramatically over the years. As the local housing values have dropped within the city limits, the surrounding urban neighborhoods have shifted from white, middle-class homeowners to a predominantly working class, ethnically diverse group of families. Mrs. Grogan has often commented to friends and colleagues that today's youngsters are entering school without the necessary level of social skills and language development. The new teachers tend to disagree with her, telling her that the students do not lack skills—that they simply do not behave and talk in the same ways that middle-class students do. Mrs. Grogan still enjoys the creativity and spirit of her students, but she believes that too often they lack respect for her authority.

Mrs. Grogan operates a very orderly yet friendly classroom. The walls are decorated with student art projects and writing samples—Halloween jack-'o-lanterns on one side and creative writing essays on the other. Her curriculum is a mix of traditional and contemporary approaches. Students meet in ability level reading groups and use basal readers. She supplements these activities with phonics lessons and children's literature.

The daily schedule in Mrs. Grogan's class moves from quiet, individual work in the early morning to more social, cooperative group activities in the later morning and afternoon. Mrs. Grogan believes that children need structure and silence in the morning to help them make the transition from the home environment to the demands of the school setting. She believes that once students settle in and become acclimated, then the activities can become more interactive and cooperative. Although Mrs. Grogan has a reputation in her school for running a very tight ship, she is also viewed as being a caring and even empathetic teacher.

Chris was transferred into Mrs. Grogan's class in late September, after he had a number of behavioral difficulties in another second-grade class. Chris had not only squirmed and turned upside down in that class, but when his teacher sent him to the office for refusing to sit upright, he called her a "bubble head" and raced out of the room. He ran out the back door of the school and lingered behind a tree at the far edge of the playground. The school principal and guidance counselor tried to first coax and then order him to return to the school building. Chris ran into the woods. He was later found playing with a dog behind a house in a nearby neighborhood.

That runaway incident spurred the principal to refer Chris for possible placement in a special education program for students with behavior disorders. The shift to Mrs. Grogan's second-grade class was suggested by the guidance counselor, who sought to find an alternative means of dealing with Chris's behavior problems.

Chris's grandfather and guardian, Mr. Stewart, fully supported the class placement change to Mrs. Grogan's room as an alternative to the behavior disorders classroom. He claimed that Chris was basically a good kid who had reacted emotionally to a number of difficulties in his life.

From birth to age 4½, Chris lived with his mother and father. Both of his parents were very involved with narcotics and alcohol abuse. The household was chaotic. Chris's parents often argued and fought. The family moved from apartment to apartment on an almost monthly basis. Chris found himself left in unknown places for hours and even days, entrusted to the uncertain care of complete strangers.

Finally, Chris's father abandoned the family, and his mother was ordered by the courts to enter a drug rehabilitation program. She asked her father, Chris's grandfather, to take care of Chris while she entered a 90-day treatment program. Otherwise, Chris would be forced into the foster care system. Mr. Stewart agreed only under the condition that she sign over permanent custody of the boy. He had watched the maltreatment of young Chris for too long and was determined to provide a permanent, stable home. At 4½ years of age, Chris moved in with his grandfather, the man who cares for him to this day. Mr. Stewart is a 58-year-old middle-school janitor who believes that a combination of strict discipline and love make for a proper, Christian upbringing. He has worked closely with the professionals at Southern Elementary to find a way for Chris to succeed.

Chris's mother currently lives in a small house three blocks away from Chris. He sees her on an irregular basis. She is still very involved with drugs. Sometimes she spends afternoons playing with and caring for Chris. Sometimes she is gone without notice for weeks or months on end.

In a meeting with the guidance counselor, Chris said that he is better off living with his grandfather, but he hopes someday that he can live with his mom. He said the reason that he cannot live with her now is because she has a disease called alcoholism that makes her do the wrong things. He says that he, too, tends to do the wrong things. He says that he doesn't know why. When the guidance counselor asked him to draw a picture of himself, he drew a boy with a straight, horizontal line for a mouth and an enormous heart that filled the entire torso. The heart was drawn upside down.

CASE 34

VALENTINE'S DAY

THE INCIDENT

As the fifth-period bell chimed through the halls of Dewey High School, Mr. Rollins searched inside his cluttered briefcase for his lecture notes and a well-worn Keats anthology. Hearing a shriek and a roar of laughter, he looked up to see a noisy huddle of students gathering at the back of his classroom.

"Just move your butt and gimme the seat," Torre demanded. Sylvia did not move. Her face was red with fear and embarrassment, and her eyes darted around as if looking for someone to save her from this menace. She turned to her friend, Elsa, who was sitting behind her. Elsa quickly supplied the necessary protection.

"Little Torre boy," Elsa jeered, "why don't you just sit up front with the rest of the hillside nerds?" The students in the back of the class laughed. Torre reached out and grabbed something from Elsa's hands. She immediately lunged forward, sprawling across Sylvia's desk and clamping onto Torre's jacket.

Mr. Rollins rushed forward and nudged his way to the center of the commotion. Torre and Elsa were tangled on the floor in a wrestling match. Elsa had Torre in a headlock. Torre was curled up in a ball on the floor. He clutched a red envelope, a Valentine's Day card, to his chest. "That's mine! Give me it!" Elsa shouted as she grabbed for the paper. Torre's body shook with laughter at her feeble attempts to take the envelope away. Repeatedly Torre said, "Whore! Whore!" The more he repeated the insult, the harder Elsa tried to pull the card from his hands.

BACKGROUND INFORMATION

Dewey High School is situated at the edge of an old working class neighborhood. The students are predominantly white. About half live in the local neighborhood. The rest ride buses from newer, more affluent areas that are building up in the surrounding hills. In the past decade, the composition of

Dewey High has changed dramatically, due to the influx of middle-class students. The growth of middle-class housing is the result of the sudden inundation of computer software and engineering companies across the hilly outskirts of town. Shiny new office parks sprang up almost overnight. The hill region was quickly developed into posh housing complexes—with gates and security guards—and new shopping areas consisting of stylish, upscale shops and restaurants.

There are tensions in town and in the high school, a general strain between the old blue-collar families and the new professional class. At Dewey High School, the working-class students are known as "townies" and the more affluent students are called "hillsiders." Some of the townies feel that their old mill town is being stolen away and modernized by outsiders who don't really care. Some hillsiders look down at the townies because of their coarse styles of dress and unrefined modes of behavior.

Mr. Rollins is a first-year English teacher at Dewey High School. While some of his colleagues grumble about the vulgar manners and language of "this younger generation," Mr. Rollins finds himself fascinated with the creativity and spirit of the adolescents he teaches. He has received some criticism from colleagues for his tendency to run a loose, wide-open classroom—that is, for allowing students too much freedom. He runs a relaxed, conversational classroom that encourages student participation. He feels comfortable with students talking out without raising hands, and he doesn't mind the students' occasionally suggestive language. Still, as a new teacher, he realizes that he needs to maintain a positive image among his professional peers. He knows this may require structuring his classes in a more traditional and fixed way.

Elsa Thompson is a 15-year-old "townie" who lives with her father and two younger sisters in an old frame house half a mile from the high school. Her parents divorced when Elsa was 11. Her father was recently laid off when the glass plant closed. He had worked at the plant for 26 years. In order to make ends meet, he now works at the hardware store during the day and moonlights as a security guard for a well-to-do hillside housing development in the evening. Elsa misses him and worries about her younger sisters, ages 7 and 9. Lacking a parental figure around the house, Elsa ends up filling in as a sort of stand-in mom. For instance, she is responsible for getting her two sisters up and off to school in the morning. She prepares breakfast, makes sure the girls are properly dressed, and walks them to the bus stop at the end of the road. These responsibilities sometimes make Elsa late for her own school day.

Elsa is a very capable English student who enjoys Mr. Rollins's class. The hallway gossips at Dewey have her pegged as a sexually promiscuous girl who too quickly leaps from one boyfriend to another. Mr. Rollins has noticed that she is often flirtatious, but he has quietly questioned the accuracy of her loose reputation. He knows that one can never know the truthfulness of rumors. He is also aware of the inequity of the sexual rumor mill, that the status of "having a reputation" is easily branded on girls and rarely on boys. He has recently noticed how frequently demeaning terms for girls and women, terms such as *whore* and *bitch*, have become commonplace in the students' hallway dialogues.

Elsa prides herself on her independence and toughness. She can match wits and trade insults with any of the boys. She dresses in a rugged style, jeans and black leather jackets. There are times when Mr. Rollins wonders whether certain boys are trying to intimidate or harass Elsa. More than once he has observed her in the school parking lot after school, smoking cigarettes and arguing with tough-looking boys. She seems to handle herself very well in difficult situations. Mr. Rollins still wonders why she puts herself in such combative situations. He also fears that there may be other, more vicious encounters in which Elsa is not able to hold her own.

Torre Fuscetta is a "hillsider." His family moved to town 2 years ago, when his father took a sales director position with a local software company. Torre enjoys being a member of the wrestling team and often wears his Dewey letter jacket to class. Although apparently an able English student, his effort in Mr. Rollins's class has been inconsistent. Mr. Rollins has consulted with Torre's other teachers and found that he tries much harder in his other subjects. When Mr. Rollins jokingly presented this fact to Torre and asked what he could do to stir the student's interest in English, Torre responded, "If you'd get rid of all the poetry and literature and writing assignments, this would be an okay class." He seems to have only a minor interest in English.

On the other hand, Torre has demonstrated great interest in Elsa. Two weeks ago, Mr. Rollins found Elsa and Tony nestled together seductively under the back stairway. He quickly rousted them and advised them to place limits on the publicly physical nature of their budding romance. In the past week, however, some of Mr. Rollins's students informed him that Elsa had jilted Torre in favor of one of the guys on the basketball team. Elsa switched her usual seat in English class to a spot far away from her ex-boyfriend. Torre did not take the rejection easily. He changed his seat also, following Elsa, shooting her angry glances when he thought the teacher wasn't looking. Elsa again changed her seat. Torre again changed his seat in response.

This shifting and re-shifting of seats has become a daily hassle as Elsa moves to get away and Torre follows in a mocking, tormenting style. Mr. Rollins does not like to assign seats to his students. He likes the students to make decisions about where to sit and how to participate. But he is losing patience with this game of musical chairs and beginning to see no other alternative. As the conflict between Elsa and Torre is obvious to all in the class, Mr. Rollins is considering a class discussion about the problem. Perhaps that would move them toward a solution. He hesitates to initiate such a conversation, though, for fear that the topic of discussion will be unduly embarrassing to Elsa or Torre. He figures that dating relationships and sexuality might be very difficult topics for this group of teenagers to discuss openly.

On the afternoon of the wrestling match, Elsa had arranged for three of her friends to save her a single seat in the corner of the classroom. Her three friends filled the adjoining seats, thereby making it impossible for Torre to sit next to Elsa. Torre badgered one of these friends, Sylvia, to give up her seat to him. As she refused to move, Torre reached for a red envelope jutting out of Elsa's notebook. He grabbed the Valentine's Day card that Elsa had purchased for her new boyfriend. Elsa leaped forward to retrieve the card, resulting in the fracas and Mr. Rollins's intervention.

CASE 35

ALL WET

THE INCIDENT

Ms. Dodd, the director of the Rhodes School, heard a child's shrieking voice echoing down the hallway. She stepped out of her office to see 4-year-old Edna running out of her classroom. The red-faced youngster was crying and panting in a flurry of anxiety. Her teacher, Ms. Springfield, chased close at Edna's heels. The director and the teacher converged on the screaming child, each adult kneeling and placing consoling hands on Edna's back and shoulders.

"There now, Edna, calm yourself down. We've got you. Everything is going to be alright," said Ms. Dodd in a soft, comforting tone. Little Edna buried her face in the director's shoulder and cried. Ms. Dodd cast a glance up at Ms. Springfield and whispered, "What happened?"

"It was Kyle Ehlenbeck," Ms. Springfield explained. "He peed on her foot."

"In the classroom?" Ms. Dodd asked with an air of mild surprise.

"Yes. I was lining them up to go to lunch, and Edna and Kyle were missing. The kids were noisy, you know, all stirred up because of the trip to the zoo this afternoon. Kyle was teasing Edna, his ugly way of saying he likes her. He's been doing that quite a bit lately. I told him to stop. He did. Then the two of them went over to the corner and started fooling around behind the wall of beanbags. I knew Kyle was giving her a hard time, grabbing at her ponytails, but I was trying to give her a chance to stand up for herself. I guess I was wrong." Ms. Springfield felt guilty.

"These things are going to happen," Ms. Dodd reassured her teacher.

"I looked away for a moment, and Edna screamed and ran out, with her sock and shoe all wet. I came after Edna, and Mr. Desco has Kyle." Ms. Springfield lifted Edna's foot and removed her wet sock and shoe.

"Do you have any idea why Kyle did this?"

Ms. Springfield shrugged her shoulders. "Hard to say exactly. He's been having a difficult week. He seems upset all the time."

By this point, Edna had become silent. Her tears had stopped, and her eyes were closed as if a short nap might make everything feel better. Ms.

Dodd passed the girl to her teacher and stood up. "Take care of Edna and send Kyle up to my office. First, I'll talk to Kyle, and then I'll call his father in to discuss this matter."

BACKGROUND INFORMATION

Rhodes School is located in a middle-class suburb of a large city. The school consists of three preschool classrooms, three kindergarten rooms, and a small day care center for infants. The program at Rhodes is based on the principles of early learning and development developed by Maria Montessori. The program is holistic and integrated in nature, emphasizing the development of social cooperation, group solidarity, independence, creativity, and students' self-knowledge.

Ms. Springfield and Mr. Desco, the classroom aide, view themselves as facilitators of child development and community activities, gently nudging and guiding children in explorations and discoveries about self and others. Their classroom is loosely structured, allowing the children many opportunities for choice in learning and play activities. The students generally get along well together. When conflicts between the youngsters do arise, neither Ms. Springfield nor Mr. Desco has much patience. They tend to become anxious and hurriedly separate children when they start to squabble. Ms. Dodd has talked to Ms. Springfield about intervening more slowly, thereby allowing the children more of a chance to work things out for themselves. Ms. Springfield understands that children need to learn to work out social disagreements, but she also feels that her teacher role requires her to run a peaceful, orderly group.

Ms. Springfield and Mr. Desco lead a class of 4- and 5-year-old youngsters. Their classroom is very busy. It is filled with colorful objects, most of which have been created by the students. Enormous box kite mobiles that look like birds and airplanes hang from the high ceiling. The floor is a scattering of small, multicolored rugs that seem to wander about the room, shifting place almost constantly. Child-size beanbags and pillows are piled up in one corner of the room. Books, hand puppets, building blocks, musical instruments, and toys line the shelves along one wall of the room. The adjacent wall is comprised of small cubby holes, where the children put their personal items. Coats hang on hooks above the cubbies. Ms. Springfield and Mr. Desco share a large desk positioned like an island in the very center of the room.

Kyle has been a student at Rhodes for over a year. Although this is the first incident in which Kyle has urinated on a peer, this is only one of a series of troubling acts of misbehavior committed by the boy in the past 3 weeks. His mood has been one of barely concealed anger that bursts forth in occasional tussles with peers over toys or a place in line. These conflicts have gotten pretty physical. Kyle has hit or bitten a classmate five times over the past 2 weeks. Each time it seemed to Ms. Springfield that Kyle lashed out with little provocation.

Ms. Dodd walked Kyle up to her office. The boy plopped himself firmly in a chair and started singing to himself. When Ms. Dodd asked him to tell what had happened in the classroom with Edna, he turned around in the seat and hid his head. He continued to sing to himself in a soft voice. Ms. Dodd allowed him to sit and sing for about 5 minutes. Once again she asked, "Kyle, I want you to tell me about what happened in the classroom."

"Edna did it."

"Edna did what?" Ms. Dodd asked. By then she was crouched on one knee in front of the lad. But Kyle refused to talk. He kept his head buried in the back of the seat and sang to himself. Realizing she was going to get nowhere with Kyle, Ms. Dodd escorted him out to the secretary's office and seated him at a large orange beanbag chair.

As in the two previous occasions, Ms. Springfield felt that Kyle's violent behavior was concern enough to warrant a call to Mr. Ehlenbeck, Kyle's father. Again this time, Ms. Dodd called Kyle's father at his office and requested that he come to Rhodes to meet with her.

Mr. Ehlenbeck is a very proud man who generally keeps his feelings close to the vest. He works as an engineer at a large defense industry corporation. In the two previous meetings with Kyle's father, Ms. Dodd clearly explained Kyle's misbehavior while emphasizing her concern with his depressed mood. She told him that while there were some minor difficulties with temper tantrums, his teachers generally view him as a happy child. She explained that over the course of the month of October, his mood shifted noticeably. He became preoccupied, worried, and sullen. He withdrew from socializing with the other children, including his two best friends. Twice Ms. Springfield found him crying quietly in a corner by himself while the other children were playing.

When Mr. Ehlenbeck arrived to meet with Ms. Dodd this third time, the director explained the nature of the incident and voiced her concerns about Kyle's behavior and angry mood. Mr. Ehlenbeck said that he had seen no problems with Kyle at home. "Sure, he's going through a bit of a tough time with Sally and me being separated, but he'll be okay." When Ms. Dodd inquired further about the "tough time," Mr. Ehlenbeck became silent. He looked up at the ceiling for a second, gathered himself, and then spoke, "Kyle does fine when he's with me, but when he's with his mother——" Mr. Ehlenbeck halted abruptly as his voice began to creak with emotion. Ms. Dodd recalled silently that the Ehlenbecks has been separated for 3 months.

"What days does Kyle spend with you?" Ms. Dodd asked.

"It varies from week to week. Sally and I each take him 2 days at a time," replied Kyle's father in a flat tone.

Ms. Dodd wrinkled her forehead quizzically. "Two days here, two days there? That's an unusual arrangement, Mr. Ehlenbeck. Most parents who are divorced——"

"We're only separated," Mr. Ehlenbeck corrected.

Ms. Dodd continued, "Most parents who are separated arrange for the child to stay with one parent during the week and one on the weekends. Switching back and forth every 2 days can be difficult on a 4-year-old child."

"Kyle's got no problem with it. The testing shows he's functioning intellectually more like a 5- or 6-year-old," Mr. Ehlenbeck countered. "He's a very grown-up little kid. And he gets to be with both of us equally. That's important. If we did it the other way, Kyle would probably only see me on weekends. That's only 2 days out of 7, under 29% of the total time. Kyle needs more time than that with his father."

"That may be true, Mr. Ehlenbeck, but what concerns me is that Kyle may feel like he is always moving, never settling in long enough to feel at home."

Mr. Ehlenbeck became defensive. "You're talking as if this is a problem at home. Kyle's behavior is fine at both my place and with his mother. He only has behavior problems here. What does that tell you?"

"Well, I think we're doing the best we can with Kyle here, Mr. Ehlenbeck. I'm just concerned that——"

Mr. Ehlenbeck interrupted, "Aren't your teachers trained to work with preschool kids? This is supposed to be one of the best Montessori schools in the county, and you're telling me you can't handle a 4-year-old boy."

Ms. Dodd paused for a moment. She could feel her anger rising. She wanted to defend her teachers and her program. She wanted to tell Kyle's father that he was wrong. She wanted to tell him that he and his wife Sally need to seek counseling for Kyle and themselves. But she also knew that she was walking a fine line. She knew that she had a very incomplete understanding of what was going on in the Ehlenbeck family. The classrooms at Rhodes, including Ms. Springfield's, were always looking to improve. She didn't want to simply throw all the blame on the parents and claim her school has no weaknesses. Her mind racing, she looked at Mr. Ehlenbeck and thought about what to say next.

CASE 36

THE WICKMAN MEMOIRS

THE INCIDENT

When Seth first met Mr. Wickman, his fifth-grade teacher, the aged and blunt-speaking veteran told the boy that he had better "work his butt off" this year if he hoped to pass. It was soon after these comments that Seth began to experience problems in Mr. Wickman's class. For example, on Seth's second day of class, Mr. Wickman asked Seth to read a section of the textbook aloud. Seth is a weak oral reader whose skills deteriorate markedly under duress. As Seth stumbled over the words he read, he noticed Mr. Wickman becoming increasingly frustrated. Seth noticed that the other students were watching Mr. Wickman's facial expressions. When Seth stopped reading and looked up from his text, he saw Mr. Wickman grimacing as if he were agonized by Seth's reading difficulties. Before Seth could finish reading, Mr. Wickman cut him off in mid-sentence and remarked in an exasperated tone, "Okay, okay, someone else needs to read." Unaccustomed to being treated in such a degrading manner, Seth broke into tears and ran out of class, a terribly embarrassing scene to an adolescent boy.

The next day, during the science lesson, Seth fought back by making goofy faces at his teacher, wildly exaggerating Mr. Wickman's facial expressions and body movements every time the man turned his back to write on the board. As the other students giggled, Mr. Wickman's anger grew. Unable to catch Seth in the act, Mr. Wickman finally held up class until someone confessed that Seth was the guilty party. In an explosive moment, Mr. Wickman grabbed Seth by the collar and assisted him down to the principal's office.

As Seth's "class clown" reputation grew among the other students, he began to imitate other teachers in his other classes. Within 2 weeks of the initial incident, Mr. Wickman was sending Seth to the office on an almost daily basis for in-school suspension (ISS). It wasn't long before his teachers began to discuss moving Seth to a more restrictive environment, that is, a full-time learning disabilities classroom.

BACKGROUND INFORMATION

Seth Hanson was first identified as having learning disabilities and Attention Deficit Hyperactivity Disorder (ADHD) in the fifth grade. It was early in the school year when his homeroom teacher, Mrs. Jones, first noticed that Seth had reading problems and was easily distracted by noises and motion. Although he excelled in math (and loved it), he displayed weak reading comprehension skills and had difficulty maintaining attention to academic tasks for long periods of time. After Anne Jones completed some informal testing and the assessment specialist completed a battery of formal testing, it was determined that Seth met the criteria to receive learning disability services in the areas of reading and written language. At roughly the same time, he was diagnosed by his family doctor as having ADHD.

Anne thought that it was strange that Seth had made it this far without being so identified because as she looked over his records she saw many of the telltale signs of a student with a serious learning problem. As his records revealed, Seth earned C's and D's in reading and other content areas, and many of his past teachers wrote that he was "inattentive," "immature," and "impulsive" in class. Despite these signs, she also knew that past teachers were reluctant to recommend borderline students for formal evaluation because of the extensive paperwork and tracking forms that had to be filed. Anne also knew that because of the small class sizes in the school, his past teachers probably were able to give Seth much individual attention. In fact, even after being identified as LD by the school, Seth was able to receive all of his support services in his regular education classes.

Through a combination of his own compensatory strategies and instructional adaptations from past teachers, for the most part, Seth was able to pass his classes. For example, Seth developed good listening comprehension skills. By the time he entered Mrs. Jones's class, he learned to master the art of listening comprehension—that is, he was able to listen to others, repeat their words to himself, and, for the most part, understand and remember. In addition, in most of Seth's elementary school classes, the teachers would have the class take turns reading the textbook aloud, yet another advantage for Seth. He could listen to passages that he would have had trouble reading. Moreover, when Seth went home in the evening, his mother or father would help him with his homework. Despite the long hours working on his homework, Seth was very diligent and would always complete each assignment. On a number of occasions, Seth would get up early in the morning to finish any homework assignments that he couldn't complete the night before. As far as Seth was concerned, school was a successful experience.

Seth's parents, Bill and Judy Hanson, loved Ann Jones. To them, Mrs. Jones was a loving, caring teacher who was always willing to spend extra time working with Seth. For Anne, the relationship was reciprocal. Anne knew that Seth would always come to school with completed assignments, and she knew that Seth's parents would always support any educational decision that she made concerning Seth's future. Through after-school meetings and Saturday morning brunches, the Hansons and Mrs. Jones became close friends. When Seth's troubles began in the fifth grade, it was Anne who received the phone call on the first day of the school year, not his fifth-grade teacher, Mr. Wickman.

As Judy Hanson explained to Anne, Seth had the bad fortune of being placed in Mr. Wickman's class. Anne had warned the Hansons about Mr. Wickman, but she tended to sugarcoat her negative description of him so as not to cause the Hansons any unnecessary worry. As Judy spoke to Anne, she asked about his reputation. Anne replied that Bill Wickman had been in the school system for a number of years and was considered a "tough" teacher. When Judy pressed Anne for more details, she finally said that Mr. Wickman had taught fifth grade for 20 years and had earned the reputation of being a cantankerous, burned-out instructor who no longer enjoyed teaching or many of his students. The school's principal repeatedly "encouraged" Mr. Wickman to retire, but the teacher stayed on because he was tenured and was only a few years away from retirement. Instead of learning science or social studies, Mr. Wickman's students often sat through long drawn-out stories about his recent divorce, the foibles of dating, and his impending retirement to the coast of Texas. Mr. Wickman was from an "old school of thought" that believed that students with learning disabilities were either "stupid" or "lazy." On more than one occasion he was overheard saying (about students with LD) that "it's all in their heads. We cater too much to these kids. All that they really need is tougher standards and strict teachers." After 30 minutes of this conversation, Anne finally managed to calm down Judy and advise her to give Seth a chance to adjust to his difficult new environment. All kids have to learn to deal with an occasional difficult teacher. Seth deserved a chance.

Two weeks later, as Anne was walking into her house, the phone rang. Again, it was Judy reporting that Wickman had made some harsh comments to Seth about "being lazy" and "getting an attitude transplant." Anne was surprised to hear the comments, but not shocked; she had heard far worse comments.

"Look Judy, maybe you had better set up an appointment with the principal and Mr. Wickman to discuss his comments," Anne urged. Judy agreed, and a meeting was set for Friday. As Friday approached, Seth began to complain about Mr. Wickman sneering at him in class.

As Judy walked into the office that Friday, her anger had reached its boiling point. As she reached to shake the hand of Mr. Pearson, the principal, she remarked, "Mr. Pearson, if my son's reports are true, this guy Wickman is a jerk."

From the corner of the room Mr. Wickman sneered and remarked, "Nice to meet you too. Oh, by the way, your son doesn't know what he's talking about."

CASE 37

LIVING IN THE WILD

THE INCIDENT

This time the police didn't simply call like they normally do. This time the two police officers showed up at the front door, rang the doorbell, and demanded to speak to Billy. When Phil, Billy's stepdad, directed them to the shed behind the house, Officers Yonger and Frecker looked at each other in amazement. "You boys can go talk to him. I need to call my wife at work and tell her what's going on here," Phil explained. Looking out the back window at the tool shed, the officers looked at each other and shook their heads.

As they approached the shed, Officer Yonger yelled out, "Billy are you in there?" As Billy opened the door, both officers peered in and saw blankets, a TV, a radio, posters on the wall, and a blue bike. "Where did you get that bike?" asked Officer Frecker.

In a nervous voice Billy responded, "I bought it off some guy."

"Uh-huh," replied Officer Yonger as he located the ID tag on the bike. "It says here that this bike belongs to Josh Moser over on Third Street!"

"Well, the guy who sold it to me told me that he just bought it off some kid," Billy blurted out, trying his best to hide his nervousness.

"Oh yeah? Do you know what happens to kids who steal bikes?" Officer Frecker asked as he reached down and patted his handcuffs.

Just then Phil reached the shed. "Maggie will be home in 10 minutes," Phil said. "Would you mind telling me what this is all about?"

"We received a report about a stolen bike earlier this morning and," pointing to the bike, "this is it," Officer Frecker said in a stern voice.

"Uh-oh," Billy remarked with a blank look on his face.

BACKGROUND

Over the past few months, Billy's parents had witnessed a noticeable change in Billy's behavior. With increased lies and more toys showing up in his possession, they began to worry that he was getting out of control. When they sent him to counseling, his psychologist suggested that he was just going through a rough teenager stage and that he needed their love and support now more than ever before. Not happy with that response, they decided to call a special education teacher at Billy's school, Norman Blackwell, to ask for his advice.

Billy's idea to live in the shed started in June, about 2 months previous, when he had the idea of camping out in the backyard. His mom, anxious to get him out of the house, thought that it would be a wonderful experience. She agreed and told him that he would first have to find his sleeping bag. As he darted up the steps, his stepfather, Phil, commented, "Maggie, you're asking for trouble. The boy will be up all night getting into trouble." Within minutes, Billy was back downstairs with his green sleeping bag slung over his shoulder.

"Mom, look what I found," Billy exclaimed.

"Well, I hope it will keep you warm enough. And don't forget a flashlight," his mother remarked. Before she finished her sentence, Billy had disappeared out the back door. With the sun nearly down, Maggie looked out the back window only to see Billy's shadowy figure setting up camp under the old hickory tree.

As Billy set up his camp he remembered to bring matches and firecrackers. Billy had no plans to sleep that night. When he saw the lights in his parents' room dim, he knew that the night was his. He had terrorized the suburban neighborhood on several previous occasions, eluding both his neighbors and the police.

Some of Billy's past pranks include tying a piece of string to a tin can and then attaching it to his neighbor's cat, placing a burning bag of human feces at his neighbor's doorstep and then ringing the doorbell, and firing bottle rockets at passing motorists. Billy also has a history of stealing toys and destroying property in the neighborhood. Tonight was going to be a big night for Billy because he was armed with four M-80s that he had bought illegally at the Army Surplus Store.

As he headed off toward Mrs. Dennison's, Billy thought to himself, "It's payback time for calling the dog catcher on Spacer." Billy was referring to the time when Mrs. Dennison, an elderly widow, called the Office of Animal Control to report Spacer, Billy's German shepherd. This incident occurred after Spacer escaped through a small hole in the backyard fence and ran off. Frustrated that Spacer had again torn up her trash, Mrs. Dennison called and reported the dog to the authorities. He was picked up, and Billy had to pay a small fine to get him back.

Marching off to Mrs. Dennison's house, Billy's anger grew as he thought about how much he hated this woman. Upon reaching her porch, he quickly lit all four M-80s simultaneously and ran off. As he dove behind some bushes, he heard the loud explosion. Within seconds, she and other neighbors looked out their windows wondering what had happened. Through the bushes, he spotted her in her pink bathrobe standing on the front porch staring down at the pieces of her shattered storm door window. A large grin swept across Billy's face. When he heard sirens, he ran for home.

By the time Billy settled into his sleeping bag, it was approaching midnight. He soon became drowsy and fell asleep. He was sleeping very soundly when he was awakened by droplets of water falling on his face. "Oh great. It's raining. Now what am I going to do?" Billy thought to himself. Then the idea came to him. "I'll sleep in the shed," he thought. He ran to the shed, only to find most of the space filled by the lawnmower and snowblower. He moved the large items out and placed them outside in the downpour. While in the shed, Billy realized that the structure would make a great little house for him. "Wow," he thought, "I could live here." In the warmth and dryness of the shed, he fell back to sleep quickly.

The next morning he awoke to his mother's voice. "Billy, where are you?" his mother yelled from her window. Too groggy to answer, he went back to sleep. It wasn't until his stepfather opened the shed door that the bright sunlight startled him awake.

"Boy, where have you been? We've been looking for you all morning!" Phil yelled. "Oh, it rained last night, and this was the only dry place that I could find," explained Billy.

"We got a call from the police asking if you were out by old lady Dennison's house last night," his stepfather barked. "There was an explosion on her porch, and they seem to think that it was caused by you."

"Dad, I was here all night," Billy responded.

"Are you sure?" Phil prodded.

"But, Dad I was sleeping all night long. How could I have done it?" Billy pleaded.

With that his stepfather slammed the door shut and yelled, "Maggie, he's down here in the shed." As his stepfather walked back to the house he thought about what he was going say to the policeman when he called him back. Spying through the shed curtains, Billy watched as his father went back into the house.

"Got your ass old lady," Billy said to himself as he giggled at the thought of the frightened old woman standing on her porch in her nightgown.

About 10 minutes later Billy smelled the pleasant aroma of bacon and eggs cooking on the stove and ran up to the house. "Oh, hi honey, how did you sleep?" his mother asked.

"Great mom," Billy answered. As Maggie was serving him his breakfast, Billy finally got up the nerve to ask, "Mom, can I sleep in the shed and kind of make it like my room?"

His mother, taken aback at first, thought about it for a few seconds and responded, "I don't see how it could hurt." Maggie thought that since it was summer, the shed might make a neat home away from home for Billy. "Besides," she thought, "it might teach him some responsibility."

Later that night Billy brought his tiny portable TV and Spacer and began to hang posters in the shed. While in the shed, he heard his stepfather yell, "You what?" from inside the house. Sensing that they were talking about him, he ran to the house. As he crouched beneath the window he listened in on their conversation. "Maggie are you nuts?" Phil asked.

"Look Phil, it might give the boy something to do this summer," Maggie blurted out. "It would be like a hobby." The next thing that Billy heard was the slamming of the front door and his stepfather grumbling something about Maggie being insane.

Phil never really liked the idea of Billy spending all of his time in the shed and occasionally would visit him to make sure that he was not getting into trouble. As the summer went on, Billy began to bring more and more items from his bedroom into the shed. Soon Billy ran an extension cord from his house to the shed to run his appliances, like his TV and radio.

As fall approached, Billy fought with his mother to allow him to use the space heater in the shed. Billy finally won out. He placed the small portable heater in the shed. Although he was getting into trouble on a more frequent basis, Maggie still allowed him to live in the shed.

It was now late September, just about the time that Josh, Billy's neighbor, got a new bike for his birthday. Josh never liked Billy and would often drive by on his new bike to taunt him. "You just wait," thought Billy, "I'll get you."

CASE 38

CHRISTMAS TIME IS HERE

THE INCIDENT

Les flashed a quick glance over his shoulder. The security guard was around here somewhere. "Come on! Come on!" he whispered forcefully to his friend Gaffer. The two 12-year-olds picked up their pace, scurrying anxiously around the corner into an alcove by the mall rest rooms. The boys leaned up against the wall and paused to catch their breath and marvel at their escape.

"That security guard is pretty stupid," chuckled Gaffer.

"I know," agreed Les. "He saw us in front of Sears, but he was too chicken to follow us through Victoria's Secret. He didn't want to go into an underwear store." As Les talked, he stuck his sticky hands into the water fountain and tried to rub the ketchup off his fingers.

"Don't be such a priss, Les-ter," Gaffer mocked his friend. "Just wipe the ketchup on your pants." Gaffer demonstrated, rubbing his fingers along the front of his jeans. Les followed suit, drying his wet hands on the back of his baggy trousers.

To their surprise, when the two boys looked up, a team of three security guards was standing in front of them. They were trapped between the guards and the three walls of the alcove. "Got any ketchup, fellas?" joked one guard as the three men took Les and Gaffer into custody. They walked the boys to the security guard station, a small office at the far end of the mall. Les and Gaffer sat quietly and stared at the tile floor. They wondered how they would ever get out of this one.

One of the security guards dialed the telephone, spoke for a few seconds, then held out the receiver.

"Who's doing the honors?" quipped the guard as he offered the phone to Les.

"Who——who is it?" asked a confused Les.

"Find out for yourself, ketchup boy." The guard pressed the telephone receiver into Les's hand and wrapped the boy's fingers around the handle. Les hesitantly pushed it against his ear. His mind filled with questions. Was it his mother? How did the guard know his phone number?

"Gaffer?" a sweet as pecan pie voice asked. It was Mrs. Kimberly, the church secretary at First Presbyterian.

"No, Mrs. Kimberly, it's me, Les."

"Now Lester," Mrs. Kimberly said, trying to fill her gentle voice with the stern air of authority—which made her sound like an uncomfortable cross between Olive Oil and George S. Patton. "Dear me. What have you boys gotten yourselves into? The Reverend Shaw is worried sick. He had to cancel rehearsal for the Christmas play, and there's only a week until the curtain goes up."

"I'm sorry, Mrs. Kimberly," Les tried to explain. "We just got bored being shepherds, you know, waiting around for Jesus to make it to Bethlehem in Act Three. There's all that waiting in Act Two, so me an' Gaff just thought we'd walked over here for a cold pop."

"Oh, Lester, the reverend is hopping mad. He's on his way over. He'll be there any minute. And he left me to call your parents. Oh dear. Now I have to call your parents and upset them."

"I know, Mrs. Kimberly. I'm sorry 'bout that."

Reverend Shaw walked into the office. The boys hung their heads. Les apologized to Mrs. Kimberly one last time and handed the telephone back to the security guard. The Reverend's usually calm and encouraging face was filled with tension. Then he sighed deeply. He seemed to go limp, his head drooping to one side and his body shrinking in exasperation. With an air of resignation, he plopped down on the chair next to the two boys. "What am I going to do with you two? We're trying to produce a Christmas play, and two of my actors are off splatting ketchup packets all over the food court of the mall. Is that any way for shepherds of the Lord to behave?"

BACKGROUND INFORMATION

Located in Hampstead, a growing suburban area, First Presbyterian Church is a growing congregation struggling to deal with a changing population of churchgoers. Historically, Hampstead had been a very settled community, a mix of small farms, old neighborhoods, and a smattering of businesses. The pews of First Pres, which were filled with the Hancocks, the Ysseldykes, the Beckfords, and the Kalks in 1965, were filled with the same group of surnames in 1975 and 1985. Generations of families remained in Hampstead. The young people went away to college and later returned to work and raise their own children in the same closely knit neighborhoods that had raised them. A certain continuity and certainty came with these patterns of community. Few newcomers entered Hampstead, and few new faces joined the congregation of First Pres. For over 30 years, a single minister and his widowed sister, Reverend Shaw and Mrs. Kimberly, directed the worship activities of First Pres.

A building boom in the early '90s changed everything. Suddenly, the small farms were sold off to developers and rows of fancy new houses sprang up across the rolling countryside. With the neighborhoods came an influx of new residents. The church rolls of First Pres nearly doubled in 5 years. An intensely proud man, Reverend Shaw refused to hire a youth minister or a music minister to help him handle the increased workload. He did it all, typically putting in a 12- to 14-hour day. The strain could be seen on his face—the pale, tight grimace of a man pushed to exhaustion—but the Reverend joked that this was merely "the Lord's anxiety," and anything with the Lord's name on it must be good.

Since mid-November, the Young Teens group at First Pres has met three nights a week in the church basement to work on the Christmas play, which is directed by Reverend Shaw. Mrs. Kimberly handles the lights and props. Les and Gaffer have relatively minor roles in the play. In fact, the two boys are typically rather inconsistent members of the Young Teens. Although the teen group meets on Wednesday evenings throughout the year for Bible study and fellowship, Les and Gaffer generally only attend during the summer months, when the group goes on recreational outings to theme parks, the zoo, and baseball games.

Les's family moved to the area and joined the church 3 years ago. Les lives with his mother and three older sisters. He and his mother attend First Pres each Sunday. His sisters, ranging in age from 15 to 19, say they are old enough to decide not to go to church anymore. Les's mother is saddened by this, but she doesn't want to fight the girls about attending services. Recently, Les has caught some of this independent attitude, and his mother has had to practically drag him out to the car every Sunday morning. In an effort to propel Les back into his faith, she asked Dr. Shaw to personally invite Les and his best friend Gaffer to participate in the Christmas play. Dr. Shaw understood the problem and agreed.

Gaffer is Mark Gaffey, the only son of an old and prominent family in Hampstead. His father owns and operates the Hampstead Homes, a string of statewide nursing care facilities. The Gaffey family have been members of First Pres since the church was founded in 1906. Gaffer's great-great-grandfather purchased and installed the original pipe organ for the church. Dr. Shaw considers the Gaffeys to be one of the pillars of his congregation. He often consults Mr. Gaffey on church financial issues.

Gaffer often feels like his father disapproves of him. This is due not so much to anything that his father says or does as much as to the lack of contact between the busy dad and the underachieving boy. Gaffer attends First Pres services every Sunday with his parents. Unlike his pal Les, he would never consider telling them he doesn't want to go to church.

While Gaffer and Les have regularly attended the Christmas play rehearsals, their efforts as actors and as group participants has been minimal. They have kept themselves separate from the nine other cast members. This act of splitting from the main group has not been openly disruptive. The boys have been compliant and polite for the most part. They just haven't said very much to the other teens.

The ages of the cast members range from 12 to 15. Les and Gaffer are the youngest and probably the most immature. Of the 11 cast members, 8 are girls. Dr. Shaw has often wondered if Les and Gaffer don't feel sexually and socially intimidated by the group of older girls. The only other boy in the cast is tall, lanky, pimple-faced Eddie Dornhauer, a slow-talking, kind-as-the-day-is-long type of boy that Les and Gaffer can't stand. He tried to befriend Gaffer but was quickly repelled. He is well liked by the girls for his kindness and sense of humor.

There was one rehearsal that Gaffer did not attend, leaving Les to fend for himself without his sidekick. Dr. Shaw was fascinated to see a very different side of Les. The usually brooding and quiet boy flirted shyly and awkwardly with the older girls. The girls seemed to take to him instantly. They found him to be charming and interesting.

The next night Gaffer was back at rehearsal. At first, the girls tried to talk and joke with Les, hoping to lure him back out into the open. He seemed caught between his loyalty for old friend Gaffer and the excitement and enjoyment of his new friends, the girls of the cast. When Les interacted with the girls, Gaffer walked off to the edge of the stage. He didn't say a word, but he was visibly upset. Soon Les fell back into his old pattern of only hanging out with Gaffer, and the girls were no longer Les's friends.

As the rehearsals progressed, Les and Gaffer found themselves waiting and watching for long periods of time. Neither boy had a line in Act Two. One night Gaffer suggested that they take this opportunity to sneak out the back door and walk over to the new shopping mall, a short quarter mile down the street. Just as the boys figured, no one seemed to miss them. They goofed around in the mall for 45 minutes and returned in time to read their lines for Act Three. After a couple of mall sneak-aways, Dr. Shaw caught on. He pulled the boys aside at the end of rehearsal one night and told them that if they left the church basement again, he would have to call their parents. The boys promised not to do it again. This promise was given a week before the ketchup incident detailed above.

On the night of this incident, the boys engaged in a brief but messy ketchup war with three other boys in the food court. Les and Gaffer claim that they fired back in self-defense. The mall security guard who witnessed the event couldn't discern who started the battle. All he knows is that he saw five boys stomping on and throwing packets of ketchup. He shouted the required, "Hey you!" and all five boys ran off, leaving behind an enormous red mess in the center of the food court. He chased the two smaller boys and caught them in the alcove by the rest rooms.